A PICTORIAL HISTORY OF WORLD WAR II IN ALASKA AND NORTHWESTERN CANADA

THE FORGOTTEN WAR

Volume FOUR

Somewhere in the Aleutians

Written by Jack Day, Captain in the Artillery,
on Kiska, January 1944

Somewhere in the Aleutians
    Where the mind is like a curse

And every day that follows
    Is always slightly worse

Where the rain and sleet blow harder
    Than shifting desert sand

And men are always dreaming of
    A fair and warmer land

Somewhere in the Aleutians
    Where women are never seen

Where the skies are always cloudy
    And the grass is never green

Where the raven's lusty screeching
    Robs a man of precious sleep

Where there's never any whiskey and
    The beer is never cheap

Somewhere in the Aleutians
    Where the mail is always late

And a Christmas card in November
    Is considered up to date

Where we always have a payday
    And never have a cent

But we hardly miss the money
    For we'd never get it spent

Somewhere in the Aleutians
    Where the trout and salmon play

And there's always a replacement
    For the one that got away

Please take me to the land
    Where the one I love doth dwell

For this God-Forsaken outpost
    Is a substitute for Hell.

VIA CLAIR DECKER, LAFAYETTE, NEW JERSEY

A typical day on Kiska—blinding fog and 50 mph wind. DENVER PUBLIC LIBRARY

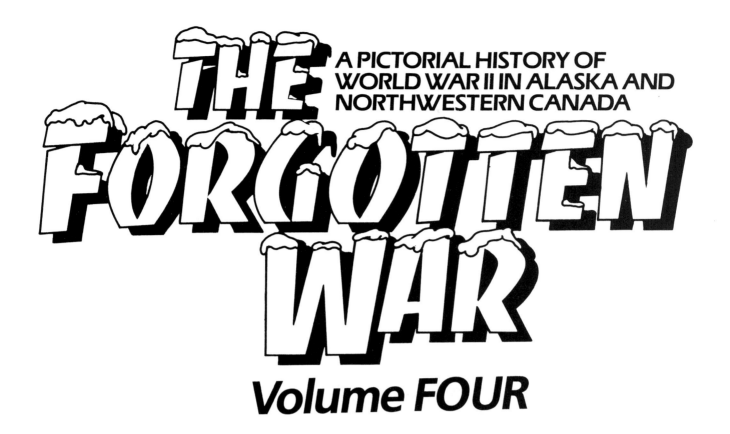

THE FORGOTTEN WAR

A PICTORIAL HISTORY OF WORLD WAR II IN ALASKA AND NORTHWESTERN CANADA

Volume FOUR

BY STAN COHEN

Aleutian Battle Ground

PICTORIAL HISTORIES PUBLISHING COMPANY
MISSOULA, MONTANA

LIBRARY OF CONGRESS
CATALOG CARD NO. 81-80570

ISBN 0-929521-64-1

First Printing: May 1993
Second Printing: April 1997
Third Printing: April 2000

PRINTED IN CANADA

Typography: Arrow Graphics
Cover Graphics: Mike Egeler, Egeler Design

COVER PHOTO:
One of the Japanese 6-inch Coast Defense guns left on Little Kiska Island.

PICTORIAL HISTORIES PUBLISHING COMPANY, INC.
713 South Third Street West, Missoula, Montana 59801
Phone (406) 549-8488 E-Mail phpc@montana.com

Introduction

It is fitting that the first printing of Volume Four of my *Forgotten War* series will be published in 1993, the 50th anniversary of the Battle of Attu and the occupation of Kiska. In the past decade I have been in communication with hundreds of veterans of the war in both Alaska and Northwestern Canada and am still amazed at the amount of information and number of photos that have surfaced. There still seems to be a great interest in this theater of operations from veterans, family members and even the younger generation.

There are numerous events going on in 1993 as there was in 1992, including a name change at Shemya Air Force Base and a ceremony in June at Attu to commemorate the battle. Several reunions of Aleutian veterans are taking place around the country.

The numbers of veterans are rapidly thinning and I hope these four volumes will perpetuate the memory of the campaign for future generations. There will possibly be a fifth volume if enough new information and photos appear in the future.

Several other books on World War Two in the area have been published and I urge my readers to seek them out.

This volume could not have been completed without the help of John Cloe, historian for the 11th Air Force in Anchorage. His articles on Gen. Simon B. Buckner and Col. William O. Eareckson were taken from his book *Aleutian Warriors*. In addition, many of the photos and captions from his book are included here. Cliff Salisbury provided the photos for the chapter on the Alaska Territorial Guard, all from his book *Soldiers of the Mists*.

Robert Gleason of Annapolis, Md., provided his story of the AACS in Alaska along with Bob Coonrad's ACS story. Stacy H. Dobrzensky of Oakland, Calif., who has been a great help with this project, provided comments of his Russian Lend-Lease experiences. Joe Rychetnik of Palm Springs, Calif., provided the story on William Thies.

In addition, I wish to thank the following for their help with articles, photos and information: Steve Levi, Anchorage, Ak.; Blaine Corneilson, Wasilla, Ak.; Harry Elegreet, Albuquerque, N.M.; Ralph Bartholomew, Ketchikan, Ak.; Donald Matheson, Duncan, B.C.; Malcolm Parks, Gig Harbor, Wa.; Thomas Niethamer, Woodland, Mich.; Everett Cooper, Spring Lake, Mich.; Harold Smith, Pocatello, Idaho; Capt. Mike Haller, Alaska National Guard; Dale Luttmann, Grand Haven, Mich.; Donald McArthur, Aberdeen, Wa.; Tom Callahan, Seward, Ak.; British Columbia Aviation Museum, Sidney, B.C.; Yukon Anniversaries Commission, Whitehorse, Yukon; Kodiak Historical Society; *The Whitehorse Star*; Warren Schmitke, Norman Wells Historical Center; James Dietrich, Sistersville, W.Va.; Joe Byrd, Lufkin, Texas; Wanda Chin, University of Alaska Museum; Benjamin M. Woods, Bronx, N.Y.; Ellen Corea, Dawson Creek Rendezvous '92; Donna Kyllo, Ft. St. John-North Peace Museum, B.C. and the staff of the Denver Public Library, Western History Department.

A further thanks to Joan Fox for proofreading, Dick Guth and Leslie Maricelli for manuscript keyboarding, Mike Egeler for cover design and Arrow Graphics for typesetting.

STAN COHEN
June 1993

PHOTO SOURCES
NA—National Archives
LC—Library of Congress
USA—U.S. Army Archives
USN—U.S. Navy Archives
USAF—U.S. Air Force Archives
AAF—Army Air Force
KHS—Kodiak Historical Society
FDR—Franklin Delano Roosevelt Library
YA—Yukon Archives
USMC—U.S. Marine Corps Archives
USNI—U.S. Naval Institute
UAA—University of Alaska Archives
ASL—Alaska State Library

Other photos are credited to their source.
Photos without credits were taken by the author or are in his collection.

Table of Contents

BACK COVER PHOTOS

Top left: 50th Anniversary ceremonies at Dutch Harbor, Alaska, June 1992. ALASKA NATIONAL GUARD

Top right: 50th Anniversary ceremonies at Soldier's Summit on the Alaska Highway, Kluane Lake, Yukon, November 1992. YUKON ANNIVERSARIES COMMISSION

Bottom: Attu Island, painted in 1879 by Henry Wood Elliott. ANCHORAGE MUSEUM OF HISTORY AND ART

BACK COVER INSIGNIA

Insignia (left to right): The Kiska Task Force patch. Approved for local wear only for troops participating in the August 1943 Kiska invasion. It was worn on both sleeves by some of the personnel involved.

Insignia of the Army Airways Communications System.

The Northwest Service Command was activated on Sept. 2, 1942, to operate and maintain the Alaska (Alcan) Highway. The colors represent both the United States and Canada. The patch was approved for wear on March 23, 1943, and the basic design of the insignia suggests a winterized pyramid tent. The star represents the North Star and the white line up the center suggests the highway.

The ATC (Air Transport Command) button. The command operated the Lend-Lease program for aircraft flown from Great Falls, Montana, through Canada to Alaska for turn-over to Russian pilots. BUTTON COURTESY DONALD MATHESON

Margaret Dinwoody of Seattle, a member of the American Red Cross, trudges through the snow to shop for convalescents at a trading post just off an army post in Alaska. With a doctor's permission she buys candy, tobacco, chewing gum and other small articles. Her parka is made of reindeer hide.
AMERICAN RED CROSS

Gen. Simon Bolivar Buckner

There were many well-known officers who participated in the Alaska and Northwestern Canada Theater of Operations but one name stands out above all others — Gen. Simon Bolivar Buckner Jr., namesake of the famous Confederate general, Simon Bolivar Buckner.

By temperament and background, the strapping, ruddy-complexioned, white-haired Col. Simon Bolivar Buckner Jr. was well suited for his first major command after 33 years of military service. The 54-year-old Kentuckian was an avid outdoorsman with an extensive academic background as a student and instructor in the Army's school system.

His father had achieved dubious fame by accepting unconditional terms from his West Point classmate, Gen. Ulysses S. Grant, for the surrender of Fort Donalson. Buckner and Grant were forever linked with the term "unconditional surrender." The Confederate general, who had once loaned a destitute Grant money, bitterly commented after the surrender, that if it had not been for his men, he would not have accepted such "ungracious and unchivalrous terms."

Following the war, Buckner senior entered politics, became the adjutant general of Illinois and later governor of Kentucky; and as a 62-year-old widower, married a 28-year-old woman and fathered his namesake. The junior Buckner, an only child adored by his father and mother, grew up in the rugged outdoors of the rolling, wooded hills of Kentucky where he developed a lifelong passion for the outdoors. Glib of tongue and quick of mind, he did well in rural schools. After almost two years at the Virginia Military Institute, Buckner received an appointment to West Point where he graduated in 1909, ranking 57th in his class of 107.

Commissioned in the infantry, Buckner served in a succession of infantry assignments where he developed a reputation as a strict but fair taskmaster. He spent World War I in the United States with the fledgling Army Air Service trying to instill a sense of discipline in would-be aviators. During this time he learned to fly, but when the war was over, he reverted back to his beloved infantry. The brief experience, however, left him with an appreciation for the potential of military aviation.

During the next 20 years, Buckner served two tours at West Point as an instructor and Commandant of Cadets, attended the Army Command and General Staff School for two years, stayed on another three years as an instructor, and graduated from the Army War College where he remained for three years as the executive officer after graduating with honors. The experience

1st Lt. Buckner in 1913 as an aide to Gen. Liggett at the 50th anniversary reunion of the Gettysburg Battle.
PENNSYLVANIA STATE HISTORICAL SOCIETY

earned him the reputation as one of the Army's leading schoolmasters and provided him a thorough theoretical knowledge of operations and tactics.

Because of this background and his rich vocabulary, Buckner's brother officers, who served in a profession not known to be very articulate, were inclined to accuse him of possessing too much surface brilliance. Buckner also suffered from a lack of tact, which did not help him in his dealings with others; and reflecting his cultural background, a racial bias towards minorities. Protesting DeWitt's plans to send a Black artillery unit to Alaska, Buckner feared their presence would "result in a serious and lasting race problem, since they will interbreed with the Indians and many of them will probably settle here." His attitude toward Alaska's Natives was not much better, much to the disgust of Governor Gruening.

Buckner's shortcomings, however, were far exceeded by his drive and dedication to building Alaska's defenses. Enjoying his newly acquired title, "The Silver Stallion of Alaska," Buckner was constantly on the move. He advocated the defense of Alaska to a fault, to the exclusion of a broader strategic view which had relegated the territory to a lower priority.

He was also an apostle of the vigorous life. While Commandant of the Cadets at West Point, Buckner was horrified to discover that some of the cadets were using cold cream and after-shave lotion. He immediately banned their use, claiming that "Cadets should work and smell like men." Buckner was hard on himself and hard on others. He handed out demerits so unmercifully at West Point that one cadet complained, "Buckner forgets that cadets are born and not quarried."

At the time of his selection to command Army forces in Alaska, Colonel Buckner was serving as the Chief of Staff, 6th Infantry Division at Fort Lewis, Washington. Lt. Gen. John L. DeWitt, Commander, IX Corps, had decided that the aggressive, outdoor-inclined Buckner was the ideal man for Alaska. The general, from his headquarters at the Presidio, California, was responsible for the defense of the western United States and the territory of Alaska. It was from his command that the forces would be drawn to garrison and defend the territory, and the general would insist on retaining operational control of the northern area long after military wisdom dictated that Alaska be made a separate theater of operations.

General Buckner remained in Alaska until June 1944, when he was assigned as the Commander, U.S. Tenth Army. He led it during the last operation of the war in the Pacific, the taking of Okinawa. He was killed in battle on June 18, 1945, when he was hit by a piece of shrapnel in the heart while at a forward command post. He was one of two three-star generals to die in battle. Lt. Gen. Lesly J. McNair, Commander, Army Ground Forces, was killed during the breakout operations from the Normandy beachhead.

A formal portrait of General Buckner by Lt. Willard Cummings, 1944. USA SC198270

General Buckner in 1944.

HEADQUARTERS ALASKAN DEPARTMENT
OFFICE OF THE COMMANDING GENERAL
APO 942 c/o Postmaster, Seattle, Washington

4 June 44

Subject: Letter of Commendation

To   : Commanding Officer,
         201st Infantry, Camp Carson.

1. I wish to express my deep appreciation to the officers and men of your organization for the outstanding devotion to duty, courage, and efficiency which they have displayed over the many months of thier assignment in the North Pacific.

2. The extremely difficult terrain and unfavorable weather conditions prevalent in Alaska and the Aleutians created manifold handicaps beyond those normally expected of troops to endure, however, your ruggedness, ingenuity and persistence enabled you to overcome all difficulties and produce outstanding accomplishments.

3. Your unceasing labors, the effective execution of your missions, and superior courage, were great factors and contributions in overpowering the enemy in the Aleutians,

4. The zeal, enthusiasm and devotion to duty by officers and men of your organization is worthy of the greatest praise and is a source of inspiration and pride.

s/ S. B. Buckner, Jr.
S. B. Buckner, Jr.
Lieutenant General, US Army
Commanding

The Viking Warrior

Except for Col. William Olmstead Eareckson, the campaigns of the North Pacific produced few heroes. In addition to earning the Distinguished Service Cross, the Navy Cross, the Silver Star and the Distinguished Flying Cross, he also won the love and admiration of those who served under him, if not the gratitude of his superiors.

The soldierly looking major, who had the build of a 175-pound halfback, celebrated his fortieth birthday four days after his arrival in Alaska, and the next two years he would leave his unforgettable mark in there. Of Viking decent, he was born in Baltimore, Maryland, and grew up on lands that had belonged to his family since 1690. His ancestors had first migrated from Sweden to England and then had accompanied Lord Baltimore in the founding of the Catholic colony in Maryland during the 17th Century. During 1914-1917, he attended St. Johns College, a preparatory school in Annapolis, Maryland, with the idea of going to West Point. However, he quit in February 1917 to join the Army. In April, the United States declared war on Germany.

The seventeen-year-old Eareckson was sent to France. However, except for a brief period when he went absent without leave to the front, the frustrated young private had to sit out the war in the rear area. Mustered out shortly after the Armistice in 1918, he reenlisted with the idea of gaining an appointment to West Point. In 1920, Eareckson finally realized his dream when he entered the Military Academy on a Presidential appointment. His cadet years were not distinguished by academic brilliance; he ranked 284 out of the 407 members of his class who graduated in 1924. He played intramural football and was on the boxing team but did not qualify for the Academy monogram. He sang in the glee club for four years and served as his class historian. When asked later on a biographical questionnaire if he had achieved any honors at West Point, Eareckson, scrawled, "Graduated!!" However, he looked back at the experience as "the most formative years of my life."

Shortly after graduation, he entered flight school at Kelly Field, Texas, where he was "washed-out" in 1925 for "inherent lack of ability to become a military aviator." Typically undaunted, Eareckson, who had listed the three choices of assignment upon graduation from West Point as "Air Corps," "Air Corps" and "Air Corps," applied and was accepted for balloon school, from which he graduated as an observer and pilot. He spent the next five years at Scott Field, Illinois, the Army Air Corps center for lighter than air operations and training. In 1928, Eareckson and Captain William E. Kepner represented the United States in the Gordon Bennett International Balloon Race. The two came in first, earning them The King Albert of Belgium Trophy and letters of commendation from the Chief of the Army Air Corps.

Eareckson, who had never given up hope of becoming an airplane pilot, was finally accepted for the second time for flight training in 1930. He was twenty-nine years old, well above the normal age for those undergoing the rigorous training. This time, however, he easily won his wings, explaining that the instructors had by then been taught to teach. He spent the next nine years as a bomber and pursuit pilot and was serving as a bomber instructor at Lowery Field when he was selected to command the 36th Bombardment Squadron.

He was a man of action who preferred the cockpit of an airplane to a desk, and an officer who strongly believed that the best way to lead was to set the example by going in "harms way." In his letters to Maj. Gen. William Butler, later to assume command of the Eleventh Air Force, Eareckson vented his frustrations over what he perceived to be too much red tape and too many unnecessary discussions.

While his men, who called him Colonel "E," revered him and his friends addressed him as Erick, his superiors referred to the impetuous Eareckson as "Wild Bill";

Col. William O. Eareckson. In May 1993 the former Shemya Air Force Base in Alaska was renamed Eareckson Air Force Station. 11TH AIR FORCE

resenting his brash, no nonsense manner, and sometimes criticized him for spending too much time in an airplane when he should have been on the ground tending to the tedious but necessary administrative and operational details that often spelled the difference between the success and failure of a mission.

Apparently reckless and independent in a profession that demanded conformity and team work, Eareckson was innovative in his tactics and a dedicated professional when it came to getting the job done. Ramputi thought him a dynamic leader, and credited him with introducing precision low-level skip bombing and forward air control procedures in the Aleutians before they became common practices in the other war theaters. Whatever his genius or faults were, Eareckson was the right person for a difficult job in a very lonely theater of operations.

Immediately upon his arrival, Eareckson took command of the 28th Composite Group, replacing Major Titus who became Major Davis' deputy. Davis' two-man command from the previous August had grown to 2,087 men by June 1. Earlier, on March 3, shortly after the redesignation of the Alaska Defense Force as the Alaska Defense Command, Buckner appointed Davis as the command's Chief of Aviation. The general also recommended him for promotion to lieutenant colonel.

An Alaska Marine, Sgt. William A. Holub of Chicago, Ill., shows his buddies a letter received from Illinois Governor Dwight Green on his recent promotion. USMC

Richard Finnie

Born in the Klondike, the son of the first Director of the Northwest Territories and Yukon for the Department of the Interior and grandson of the founder of the Dawson Daily News, Richard Sterling Finnie had the North in his blood.

At seventeen, he served as a radio operator under the famous Captain J.E. Bernier on board the *Arctic*. Voyages in the mid-1920s took him far north to the tiny outposts and whaling stations among the islands of the Eastern Arctic. Thanks to several fellow crew members who had expertise in photography and journalism, Finnie learned the basics of motion-picture filming and production.

He put his new skills to good use several years later, when he was appointed historian to the Canadian Government Eastern Arctic Expeditions. His first film, *In the Shadow of the Pole*, is a record of the 1928 voyage of the S.S. *Boethic*. It features the hustle and bustle of an outport at "ship time," when new provisions are unloaded at the docks. Over the next 10 years, he produced a variety of films and wrote several books on the North.

Thanks to his knowledge of the North and his film-making experience, the U.S. Army Engineers retained Finnie's services in 1942 to document the construction of the Alaska highway and pipeline. As part of this massive project, Finnie produced some 45 reels of film and thousands of still photographs. Its success resulted in an invitation from the international engineering giant Bechtel to serve as company historian and film producer. Over the next quarter century, Finnie produced more than 60 films documenting projects in all corners of the globe. He often served as his own cameraman, writer, director, soundman and narrator.

Richard Sterling Finnie died in 1987. His collection of films, photographs, manuscripts and sound recordings was donated to the National Archives of Canada by his wife. It contains some of the most impressive film footage ever taken of life in Canada's North.

Reprinted from the Klondike Sun, *Dawson City, Yukon.*

The Whitehorse Star

CIRCULATING THROUGHOUT THE YUKON TERRITORY

Vol. 42.   No. 50.   ★ ★ ★   WHITEHORSE, YUKON, FRIDAY, DECEMBER 11th, 1942.   ★ ★ ★   Subscription $3.00 Year.

SADDEST AIRPLANE TRAGEDY IN HISTORY WHITEHORSE IN WHICH THREE LIVES ARE LOST.

A week ago today there occurred the saddest fatal accident so far in the history of Whitehorse when a Norseman plane, piloted by Les Cook and accompanied by his two mechanics, Ken McLean and Don Dickson, crashed on one of the main streets near the home of Mr. and Mrs. I. Taylor.

It was shortly after 4 o'clock in the afternoon when the trio left the local airport on a test flight. That the flight was intended to be of short duration was evidenced by the fact that the engine of their motor truck was left running at the airport due to the low temperature prevalent at the time. The plane had not been in the air many minutes when a forced landing became inevitable. In its descent it struck several trees as well as some telephone poles and wires in the vicinity of the hospital and upon striking the ground burst into flames. Owing to this the aeroplane and its occupants, that of Ken McLean, was extricated from the flaming inferno. The others were not secured for some hours afterwards.

A military funeral service was held at Christ Church Monday for the late Les Cook and Don Dickson. The remains of Ken McLean have been shipped to Edmonton where his widow is at the present time.

The service was conducted by the Rev. L. G. Chappell, Rector of Christ Church, assisted by two U. S. Army chaplains, Capt. Erwin T. May and Lieut. F. H. Austin, both of the Engineers Corps. The mourners were Mrs. Lillian Cook, her mother and father, Mr. and Mrs. Murray, the late pilot's father who arrived from Pincher Creek, Alberta, Mrs. Amelia Dickson, Mr. and Mrs. Dave Wilson and Mrs. John Phelps. The Guard of Honor was composed of officers from army headquarters. The pallbearers for the late Les Cook were Major Stann, Capt. Gee, Capt. Palfreyman (representing the U. S. Army) and Dr. F. Burns Roth, W. Gordon, Jr., and John Phelps. Those for the late Don Dickson were Corpl. Barry Allan, R.C.M.P., Jack Barber, Yorke Wilson, Gordon Armstrong, H. D. Zeiser and Bob Bockler (representing the Northwest Air Lines.) Both caskets were draped with the Union Jack and Stars and Stripes and an array of floral tributes whilst the firing squad was composed of an equal number of white and colored troops of the U. S. Army. It was a most impressive service, the church being filled to capacity by the sorrowing friends of the deceased.

In the name and on behalf of the

General Alexander—C in C— Middle East (left) and Lieut.-General Montgomery who took the Third Division to France in 1939.

ALL COLORED REVIEW SCORES BIG HIT WITH ARMY AT LOCAL THEATRE

A grand evening of fun was afforded the soldiers stationed in this vicinity last Sunday night when an all-colored troupe of soldier-thespians put on a show at the local Whitehorse Theatre for the Army personnel and their wives and sweethearts.

A fine array of talent was presented by the Army and included such acts as vocalists, comedians, dancers, jitterbugs and imitators and a swing trio that had the house tapping and swaying in time to its rhythm. Each performer was an artist in his own right when it came to displaying talent.

The soldier-packed audience was particularly impressed when one soldier, an imitator, gave his impression of the Amos 'n Andy radio show. This performer was the show-stopper.

Prizes were given the best acts and a grand prize was given to the act that proved to be the best of the evening. All the prizes were of the goofy "gag" type—but the first prize. It is no military secret that the grand prize was a FURLOUGH. However three men deadlocked for the grand prize, and since they were all so good, the Sector Commander, who was in attendance at the show, decided that to give just one furlough out would be cheating the other two—so all were elated when the sector commander awarded the grand prize to all three men.

wide circle of friends of the deceased, both near and far, we extend to the bereaved ones sincerest and heartfelt sympathy.

MISS B. S. HAWKINSON SENIOR NURSE IN P.R.Afl HOSPITAL IN WHITEHORSE

(By Lt. R. L. Neuberger)

An Edmonton girl, Miss Bertha S. Hawkinson of 12122 Ninety-Fourth Street of that city, holds the distinction of being the first nurse ever to work on the 1,650-mile Alcan International Military Highway, which was recently dedicated at Kluane Lake.

Miss Hawkinson is now senior nurse at the U. S. Public Roads Administration Hospital at Whitehorse, where she works under the direction of Captain O. B. Doyle, physician of the American Government's Public Health Service.

Miss Hawkinson is the daughter of Mr. and Mrs. N. Hawkinson of Mayerthorpe, Alberta. She took her training at Edmonton General Hospital with the Gray Nuns and has been at Whitehorse since last summer. She is one of the most proficient amateur photographers at this frontier settlement. Recently she photographed Brigadier General James A. O'Connor and other staff officers of the Northwest Service Command.

"This has been a great experience," Miss Hawkinson recently said of her work at Whitehorse. "The Highway is a historic undertaking and one feels proud to have been of assistance in its construction. All of us at the PRA hospital are glad of a chance to minister to the ills and sickness of the men building this great road."

Miss Hawkinson is senior nurse at the PRA hospital and is the first nurse to be employed on the Alcan Highway.

NEW FEEDER ROAD CONNECTING HAINES WITH ALCAN HIGHWAY NOW UNDER CONSTRUCTION

Brigadier General James A. O'Connor, commanding the Northwest Service Command, has informed Anthony J. Diamond, Alaska's veteran Delegate in Congress, that construction has started on a second road to connect the Alcan International Military Highway with the waters of the Inside Passage.

In a letter to Delegate Diamond, General O'Connor today declared, "I am well aware of your long-time interest in the development of land communication with Alaska. The Haines-Champagne road, construction of which has started, will connect southeastern Alaska with the Alcan Military Highway, and will be an important step in the development of the Alaskan road network. We already have landed crews and equipment at Haines.

"This road will provide a second port of entry from southeastern Alaska to the Alcan Highway and will bring the Highway closer to such Alaskan cities as Juneau, Ketchikan and Sitka."

The road will extend approximately 142 miles from Haines on the Alaskan seacoast, to the Yukon frontier settlement of Champagne. It will ascend the heights of Chilkat Pass, the third route that the '98's followed to the Klondike, the others being the Chilkoot and White of dreadful memory. Forty-two miles of the road already have been developed to some extent by the Alaska Road Commission.

The Haines "cut-off" has long been favored by Governor Ernest Gruening of Alaska. He conferred with General O'Connor concerning the new development here early in November. Delegate Diamond has also been actively urging the linking of the Alcan Highway to various parts of Alaska through the construction of additional "feeder" roads.

General O'Connor's statement was contained in a letter thanking Delegate Diamond for the message praising American workmanship on the Alcan Highway which he sent to the ceremonies opening the the road at Kluane Lake November 20.

Mrs. "Ma" Simmons of Carcross fame and the apple of her eye, George, president of Northern Airways Ltd., were in town on a short trip this week—and we missed 'em. The Dowager Duchess had "Gone with the wind" before we knew of her whereabouts. We were however more fortunate in meeting her daughter the Lady Gladys last week.

Scenes at Dutch Harbor from James C. Dietrich, member of the 264 Sep. Coast Artillery Battalion which was formed at Fort Warden, Washington, for the harbor defense of Dutch Harbor.

The band of the 206th Coast Artillery at Dutch Harbor and Master Sgt. D.L. Jones spending some leisure off-duty time. EVERETT COOPER

1st Platoon A.T. Co. 201st infantry, leaving Kodiak for Adak, November 1942. Note that they are still wearing World War I era helmets. KHS CHARLES CUM COLL.

The Russian cemetery on Amchitka at the time of the American occupation. KHS

This trapper's cabin was the only structure on the island of Adak at the time of the American occupation. KHS

II-12 GENERAL VIEW OF AREA WITH DOCK IN RIGHT MIDDLE GROUND TAKEN LOOKING IN-
board from viewpoint K.

Akutan Island during the war. The processing plant built before the war was leased to the U.S. Navy which rebuilt the dock and used it for refueling Russian freighters. At the end of the war the property was returned to its original owners but the plant was outdated and eventually burned to the ground. UNIVERSITY OF WASHINGTON, SPECIAL COLLECTIONS DIVISION, UW 14379

This B-17 crashed in Lake Bennett near Carcross, Yukon, during the war. YA, PRESTON COLL.

ATTU SUN EXTRA

FLEET SMASHES MATSUWA
-KURILE BASE BELIEVED KO'D

SURPRISE ATTACK CARRIED OUT IN ROUGH WATERS

(WITH THE NORTH PACIFIC FLEET OFF MATSUWA, 22 NOVEMBER - (SPECIAL) BY FRANK STURDY TO THE CHICAGO TRIBUNE, CHICAGO)

"NOW, HEAR THIS," A BRASSY VOICE CAME OVER THIS CRUISER'S LOUD SPEAKER SYSTEM IN THE NAVY'S TRADITIONAL COMMAND FOR ATTENTION TO AN IMPORTANT ANNOUNCEMENT. "NOW, HEAR THIS - THIS TASK FORCE WILL SET A COURSE FOR MATSUWA, AND IF WEATHER CONDITIONS ARE FAVORABLE, WILL CARRY OUT A BOMBARDMENT" THE JOB SET THIS TASK FORCE OF THE NORTH PACIFIC FLEET, WHILE CRUISING IN MID-PACIFIC THREE DAYS AGO WAS COMPLETED TONIGHT. MATSUWA WAS TROUNCED WITH MORE THAN 300,000 POUNDS OF SHELLS. HUGE FIRES WERE SET IN THE TWO-MILES SQUARE TARGET AREA. AS THE FORCE TURNED TAIL AND SPED SWIFTLY TO SEA WHEN BOMBARDMENT ENDED, NUMEROUS EXPLOSIONS SENT FLAMES KNIFING HIGH INTO THE SKY, AND AT LEAST FOUR BIG FIRES BURNED STEADILY, STILL VISIBLE WHEN THE FLEET HAD LEFT THE ISLAND AN HOUR BEHIND.

AS FAR AS COULD BE TOLD, THE ATTACK TOOK THE JAPS BY SURPRISE. THERE WAS ONLY WEAK AND INEFFECTIVE RETURN FIRE FROM THE BEACH. THE SHIP'S RADAR PICKED UP SURFACE TARGETS APPROACHING FROM THE REAR, PRESUMABLY TORPEDO BOATS, BUT TOWERING SEAS AND A SIXTY KNOT WIND PREVENTED THEM FROM CLOSING TO SHOOTING RANGE. THE FLEET ESCAPED WITHOUT BATTLE DAMAGE.

THE RAID WAS A DARING THRUST ACROSS THE NORTH PACIFIC FROM THE FLEETS ALEUTIAN ISLAND'S BASE, CARRIED OUT WITHOUT AIR COVER EXCEPT FOR PROTECTION DURING THE FIRST HALF OF THE DISTANCE BY LIBERATOR BOMBERS OF THE ELEVENTH AIR FORCE. WEATHER WAS THE FLEETS ONLY PROTECTION, WEATHER BAD ENOUGH TO PREVENT DISCOVERY BY JAP BOMBERS.

MATSUWA LIES AT ABOUT THE MIDDLE OF THE KURILE ISLANDS, 450 MILES NORTH OF THE TIP OF THE JAPANESE HOME LAND AND 850 MILES FROM TOKYO. THE JAPS HAVE USED IT AS A MAIN STAGING BASE FOR AIRCRAFT TO PARAMUSHIRO AT THE NORTH END OF THE CHAIN.

FOR TWENTY FOUR HOURS BEFORE STRIKING AT THE ISLAND'S RUNWAYS, HEAVY HOARD FUEL AND AMMUNITION DUMPS, THE TASK FORCE ZIG-ZAGGED IN ROUGH WATER 150 MILES OFF SHORE WAITING FOR LOWERING SKIES. WHEN REAR ADMIRAL JOHN MCCREA, COMMANDING THE FORCE FROM ANOTHER CRUISER SIGNALLED THE DECISION TO RUN IN, THE HEAVIER SHIPS AND THE PROTECTING SCREEN OF DESTROYERS HEADED FAST FOR THE TARGET FROM THE SOUTHEAST.

SEVERAL HOURS AFTER DARK THE FLEET BEGAN ITS BOMBARDMENT RUN, PARALLELING THE SHORE AT A DISTANCE OF ABOUT SEVEN MILES, UNDER A LOW CEILING BUT WITH VISIBILITY THAT WAS ALMOST TOO GOOD. FROM AN OBSERVATION POST HIGH ON THE FOREMAST OF THIS CRUISER, I COULD SEE THE SALVOS OF SHELLS ARCHING RED-TAILED TO THE BEACH BURSTING ON THE BLACKED-OUT TARGET.

WITHIN A FEW MINUTES THE FIRST FIRE FLOWERED IN A GREAT BALL THAT GREW STEADILY THROUGHOUT THE TWENTY MINUTE BOMBARDMENT, APPARENTLY A FUEL TANK FARM. BELOW DECKS, SWEATING GUN CREWS HEARD A DESCRIPTION OF THE BLASTING FROM TALKERS ON DECK AND CHEERED AS THEY HEAVED SHELLS AND POWDER BAGS.

THE RAPID FIRING DESTROYERS RAN IN SHORE OF THE CRUISERS, THE FORCE FORMING AN ARC OF DESTRUCTION ALONG MATSUWA'S SHORE IN A FIRING RUN OF TWENTY MINUTES.

WITH THE ORDER TO CEASE FIRE, THE FLEET HEADED STRAIGHT AWAY FROM MATSUWA AT NEARLY TOP SPEED, BREASTING A RAGING SEA. OUR FAST CRUISER BUTTED, STAGGERED TO THE TOPS OF THE HUGE WAVES, PLUNGED TO THE TROUGHS. WITH THE PROW SPANKING THE WATER IN A THUNDEROUS BOOMING. ONCE THE BOW PLOWED TWENTY FEET UNDER AN ENORMOUS COMBER. THE GIANT SEAS ROLLED THE SHIP AS MUCH AS 35 DEGREES ON HER SIDE, CLOSE TO THE DANGER POINT FOR CAPSIZING.

CAPTAIN C. A. RUMBLE AND THE OFFICERS ASSISTING HIM IN THE PILOT HOUSE WERE ANKLE DEEP IN WATER, AND THOUGH THEIR STATION IS 55 FEET ABOVE THE WATER LINE, CRANED THEIR NECKS TO LOOK UP AT THE TOPS OF THE WAVES, ESTIMATED TO HAVE REARED 70 FEET AT THEIR GALE BLOW CRESTS. THOUGH THIS NIGHTMARE OF TUMBLING TONS OF SLAT WATER AND SHRIEKING WINDS, THE HALF FROZEN CREWS OF THE ANTI AIRCRAFT GUNS ON THE MAIN DECK FOUGHT TO KEEP FROM BEING SWEPT OVERBOARD.

THE MUCH SMALLER DESTROYERS WERE IN WORSE PLIGHT. WITHIN AN HOUR ADMIRAL MCCREA WAS FORCED TO ORDER REDUCED SPEED FOR THE ENTIRE FLEET TO SAVE THEM FROM SEVERE, PERHAPS FATAL DAMAGE. THERE WERE TIMES WHEN THE FORCE ONLY MADE A FEW KNOTS. MORNING CAUGHT THE SHIPS STILL FIGHTING THE SEAS WITHIN RANGE OF JAP BOMBING PLANES, SAVED FROM POSSIBLE ATTACK BY LOW CEILING AND RAIN SQUALLS THAT CUT VISIBILITY TO LITTLE MORE THAN A MILE.

THE STORM PERSISTED THROUGHOUT THE CRUISE BACK TO BASE, BUT THE ENTIRE BATTERED FLEET MADE PORT SAFELY AND IN FORMATION.

A HARD-HITTING TASK FORCE OF CRUISERS AND DESTROYERS BLASTED A HOLE IN JAPAN'S NORTHERN FLANK TONIGHT. THEY SHELLED MATSUWA ISLAND IN THE CENTRAL KURILES, 960 MILES FROM TOKYO.

IT WAS THE MOST DAMAGING BLOW THUS FAR TO THE STRING OF ISLAND-BASES GUARDING THE EMPIRES BACK DOOR.

HUGE FIRES KINDLED IN FUEL AND AMMUNITION DUMPS SENDING PILLARS OF FLAMES SKYWARD, SETTING OFF EXPLOSIONS VISIBLE AN HOUR AFTER OUR SHIPS HEADED HOME.

RETURN FIRE FROM SHORE BATTERIES WAS WEAK AND INEFFECTIVE. JAP SURFACE AND AIRCRAFT DID NOT ATTEMPT TO INTERCEPT, AND OUR SHIPS SUFFERED NO CASUALTIES AND NO BATTLE DAMAGE.

THE TASK FORCE WHICH HIT THE JAP HOMELAND IN THE WAR'S CLOSEST SURFACE STRIKE TO TOKYO COMPOSED UNITS OF VICE ADMIRAL FRANK JACK FLETCHER'S NORTH PACIFIC FLEET. IT WAS COMMANDED BY REAR ADMIRAL JOHN L. MCCREA OF MARLETT, MICHIGAN.

THE RAID ALSO WAS THE LONGEST SURFACE STRIKE WITHOUT FULL AIR COVER. WARSHIPS HAD AN UMBRELLA OF ELEVENTH ARMY AIR FORCE LIBERATORS PART WAY, BUT PENETRATED DEEP INTO ENEMY WATERS ALONE. THEY CAUGHT THE JAPS BY SURPRISE SEVERAL HOURS AFTER SUNDOWN.

STEAMING PAST TAGAN POINT, THE SOUTHEAST TIP OF THE ISLAND, CRUISERS AND DESTROYERS POURED 150 TONS OF DESTRUCTION INTO A TWO MILE SQUARE TARGET AREA IN TWENTY MINUTES OF FURIOUS SALVOS.

FROM A BOX SEAT HIGH IN A CRUISER'S FOREMAST, I SAW HEAVY SHELLS ROCKET SHOREWARD, AND HEARD THE CREW CHEER AS TARGET AFTER TARGET UPLIT LIKE KNOBS IN PINBALL MACHINES. ONE MINUTE THE JAP ISLAND WAS DARK AS A TOMB, THE NEXT IT LIGHTED BY AT LEAST FOUR BIG FIRES AND MANY SMALLER ONES WHICH MUSHROOMED HUNDREDS OF FEET AIRWARDS. THIS INDICATED DIRECT HITS ON FUEL STORAGE TANKS.

AS THE TASK FORCE SWUNG FROM THEIR TARGET, MATSUWA'S MILE HIGH MOUNT FUJO SILHOUETTED A BLOW OF FLAMES, FANNED BY A FIFTY KNOT GALE.

THIS BOMBARDMENT WAS THE FOURTH AGAINST THE KURILES SINCE 4 FEBRUARY AND THE SECOND AGAINST MATSUWA, WHICH FIRST WAS SHELLED 13 JUNE. IN ALL FOUR STRIKES THE JAPS NEVER SUCCEEDED SCORING A HIT ON A SINGLE AMERICAN SHIP.

MATSUWA LIES MIDWAY IN THE KURILE CHAIN, 350 NORTH OF HOKKAIDO, AND THOUGH ONLY SIX MILES LONG BY A HALF AS WIDE IT IS THE KEY BASTION OF JAPAN'S NORTHERN DEFENSES. IT IS BELIEVED THE DESTRUCTION RESULTING FROM THIS SHELLING MAY HAVE NEUTRALIZED THIS BASE FOR SOMETIME AND DISRUPTED AIR OPERATION IN THE NORTH PACIFIC.

Another raid on Matsuwa by Task Force 92. The correspondent was George McWilliams of the International News Service (INS). JOE BYRD

Attu Island Air Base, Alaska
77 Bomb Squadron, 11th Air Force

October 1944

This October day a force of B-25 planes of the 77 Bomb Squadron crossed the north Pacific to hunt shipping around the most northern islands of the Japanese Kurlie Islands. As they approached the air base on the southern end of Paramushio, a perfect day with unlimited visibility, they observed a large cargo ship unloading in the small harbor behind the airfield. As this flight flew within several miles, they observed two levels of several dozen Japanese Zero fighters circling the base and harbor area, standing guard for any American planes that might try to attack this ship during unloading operations.

Being so heavily outnumbered with no chance for a surprise attack, the B-25 flight returned to base rather than try a suicidal mission with these odds against them. Upon arriving back at base, two crews from this flight volunteered to try and sink the ship by leaving Attu in the middle of the night, so as to arrive at the crack of dawn, hoping to gain a surprise advantage and even out the odds of flying a successful mission.

Lt. Douglas Banker and Lt. Andrew Goller took off at 2:00 AM during the dark of the night, flying at 500 feet over the north Pacific, using radar altimeters to stay low over the ocean surface. They flew this way for the first 900 miles, almost four hours, then they dropped down to 100 feet above the water to keep under any radar that the Japanese might have to detect their approach. During this flight, radio silence was maintained; only the planes' blue running lights were used so they could keep sight of each other and maintain a loose formation. These blue formation lights could not be seen from any great distance. As Goller and Banker approached the target area, four hours plus in time of flight, they had been briefed that they might run into a heavy weather front, reported by the Russians, to be coming in from the northwest and it may well be there before they arrived.

The lead navigator—Bombardier on Goller's plane—called over the intercom that estimated time of arrival was up, visibility was now down to just several hundred yards and very hazy. Lieutenant Goller began to wonder if they had left the air base too soon to arrive at the break of dawn as some visibility was needed to make the attack. Time and distance were critical now; the Japanese air base and harbor sat at the south end of a 4,000-foot mountain range, just a couple miles away from both installations. Goller broke radio silence to Banker, asking if they could see any reference point, for they had drifted five miles north of their destination and could easily fly into the mountains that rose straight up from the sea. Also, there had been no reference points from the time the flight left Attu and as they approached

the target area under the overcast sky that had enveloped the area for the last 50 miles. Seconds after Goller broke radio silence, a red light flashed off to the right and ahead of the planes' flight path.

Goller and Banker turned right to where the light had come from, only then realizing they were crossing a beach onto land. Both planes, battle-ready, opened bombay doors, full throttle, flying just above the rooftops of the air base—a real plus foe dropping bombs as you couldn't miss at this altitude of 50 feet. Then a large ship took shape less than a half mile ahead. A couple bursts of machine gun fire woke up the air base, but the real target was still the ship. Goller called to Banker over the radio, "Watch out for that radio pole up ahead." "No sweat," Baker called back, raising a wing and clearing it by inches.

The two planes, now side-by-side crossed into the harbor area and covered the cargo ship with .50-caliber gunfire to keep the ship's crew from reaching their gun turrets, as men were coming on deck through cabin doors.

Approximately 400 feet before crossing the ship, both planes released their 400-500-pound delayed fuse bombs (skip bombs) and climbed almost straight up to clear the ship's mast, as it was empty and riding high in the water. As the planes cleared the mast, the bombs went off, literally lifting the big ship out of the water—a beautiful sight reported by both crews' tail gunners.

As the planes leveled off from their bomb run, there was the Russian weather front, not a mile behind the Japanese target ship, a solid wall in the dawn's early light.

Goller and Banker pulled up in a formation wing-over, turning sharply to the left to avoid flying into the weather front. As they turned, they spotted two Japanese tug boats holding anti-submarine nets across the mouth of the harbor. Lieutenant Banker dove on the left tug boat and Goller strafed the right boat. Pulling up but a few feet above the water, both planes continued south out to sea, before turning left 120 degrees for home.

As the crews looked back at the Japanese air base, it was lit up like a 4th of July celebration. Gunners were firing tracers randomly in the air, probably not aware of what happened.

After flying this 1,000-mile mission, we realized if the Japanese cargo ship had not used a red light to try and alert the air base of our presence in the area—after picking up the radio transmission between Goller and Banker—we would have never spotted the air base and ship, and would have flown right on by our target. Four hours later both crews landed safely at home base without a scratch.

—*Capt. Andrew Goller, Arrowsmith, Illinois*

A Parade in Juneau, Alaska, July 1942

Harold Smith, Sgt. ACS

Members of the 75th (AA) Coast Artillery at their listening post, Fort Richardson, July 6, 1941.

ASL, U.S. ARMY SIGNAL CORPS COLL.

CHAPTER TWO

THE ALASKA HIGHWAY

Timely News Treat of the War in Far East • **CHINA'S ROAD TO VICTORY!** Latest photographs of Generalissimo Chiang Kai-Shek, his famous wife, Mai Soong Kai-Shek, and fabled Burma Road, built with the life blood of Cathay, shown in three striking picture pages, one in full color. • Read It in Today's Pictoral Review

U. S. RUSHING ALASKA ROAD

CHARACTER · QUALITY · AMERICA FIRST · ACCURACY · ENTERPRISE
Seattle Post-Intelligencer
AN AMERICAN PAPER FOR THE AMERICAN PEOPLE
Entered as Second Class Matter at Seattle, Wash.
VOL. CXXII, NO. 61 SEATTLE, MAY 3, 1942 B SUNDAY 10c

MISSING FLYER REPORTED IN WAR

FRIENDS HOPE LONG LOST HEIR NOW IN CHINA

'Andy' Whitfield, Nephew of Mrs. Andrew Carnegie, Disappeared in Airplane

(By Universal Service)

NEW YORK, May 2.—One of society's strangest disappearance mysteries seemed on the verge of solution recently with the report that rich young Andrew Carnegie Whitfield, nephew of Mrs. Andrew Carnegie, is serving under another name with a United Nations flying corps.

No official confirmation of the rumor could be obtained, however. Consequently, the true whereabouts of the dashing young aviator and heir to millions, remained as dense a puzzle today as it has been ever since, four years ago last month, he phoned his bride of a year a hasty good-by, and, climbing into his private plane, literally vanished into thin air.

But his friends would not be surprised if it turned out, as reported, that the missing man is actually engaged somewhere in knocking Nazi or Jap planes out of the sky. Knowing him as a daring flyer and a skilled marksman, they feel that "Andy" would be an addition to any aviation combat unit.

PAID FOR PLANES SHOT

One spot where he might be is in China with the "Flying Tigers" of Gen. Claire L. Chennault, volunteers who are paid $500 every time they bring down a Jap plane. At the time this group — officially known as the American Flying Volunteers — was organized, much secrecy surrounded the identities of its personnel, which would have fitted in with Whitfield's apparent determination to remain a forgotten bridegroom.

On the other hand, it is conceded the rumors may all be wrong, and that the namesake of Andrew Carnegie may merely be hiding out in the backwoods of Virginia, waiting for another year to elapse, so that his erstwhile bride, the former Elizabeth Halsey of New York, can obtain an "Enoch Arden" divorce. That was his announced intention, she says, when following a domestic quarrel, he vanished out of her

(Continued on Page 5, Column 1)

Canada May Get Free Raid Insurance

Bill Would Provide Up to $3,000 for Damage

OTTAWA, Canada, May 2.—(I.N.S.)—Canada has taken steps to meet the risk of enemy air raids. A government bill for free automatic insurance for house owners against war damage up to $3,000 has been introduced in the house of commons. The bill also provides against loss of chattels to a limited maximum and authorizes government insurance on larger properties to a maximum of $50,000. On these large properties, premiums will be paid.

Montana Campus To Show Stock

BOZEMAN, Mont., May 2.—The annual 1942 Little International Livestock Show will be held at Montana State College May 8 and 9, with Walter O. Davis of Bozeman and Al Ralston of Glasgow as managers.

Both are seniors at the college, Davis serving as publicity manager for the event last year and Ralston acting as ringmaster.

This year's Little International will mark the twelfth consecutive year that the show has been a campus feature.

Plane Vibrations Harvest Pecans

GUNTER FIELD, Ala., May 2.—When the big bombers start warming up, Corp. John E. Anglin is likely to slip out to a big tree that stands in front of his barracks.

Then when the heavy planes rumble into the sky he scoops up the three or four hatfuls of pecans that are shaken from the tree by the vibration.

BRITISH WAR ON AXIS SUBS FROM SECRET PORT

Battles of Atlantic Charted On Illuminated Wall Map in Hidden Underground Cellar

A WESTERN BRITISH SEAPORT, May 2.—(I.N.S.)—Deep in an underground cellar in this seaport town there works a staff of men and women of the Royal Navy, Merchant Navy, Air Force, and WRENS. Across the face of a gigantic illuminated wall map they move, at four hour intervals, small gaily colored markers which indicate the positions of all ships known to be at sea.

These men and women plot the course of the convoys and the isolated ships which run precious war goods and food to England from North America and the Colonies. Graphically moving together on this chart may be seen symbols representing the Allied merchantmen and the Axis U-boats, and many sensational incidents in the Battle of the Atlantic have been foretold hours in advance by these movements on the map.

This is the office and workshop of Admiral Sir Percy Noble, commander of the Western Approaches—whose "front porch" has been considerably widened this spring by the Axis U-boats which are operating off the Atlantic Coast of the United States and Canada.

SECRET LOCATION

From the outsides, this vital command center closely resembles any of the dozens of small shipping offices in the neighborhood. Through several different entrances pass the uniformed men and women who work here, however, so that none but those with official business may know the exact location of this office.

Inside, Admiral Noble's headquarters closely resembles those of the various Royal Air Force commands. His personal office and workroom is separated from the chart room by a thick wall of glass, and without moving from his desk he can tell at a glance the position of any chosen ship on the Atlantic and also the positions of known enemy craft which might be nearby.

DESCRIBED BY VISITOR

A recent visitor to this amazing headquarters—his name must remain a secret for security reasons—describes the scene as follows:

"From his desk, sitting at right angles to the huge glass window that stretches across the room, sits Admiral Noble. He did not look out upon the Atlantic as did some of his early predecessors, but looked instead upon the great wall map, half above the floor of the workroom, half below. The chart was the same gray-green as the Atlantic, and on it could be seen assorted symbols representing every convoy, every escort

(Continued on Page 5, Column 6)

NEW HIGHWAY IS VITAL NEED IF JAPS INVADE PACIFIC COAST

Work Speeding Day and Night On Corridor Through Canada That Will Cost $25,000,000

By George C. Porter

EDMONTON, Alberta, May 2.—(I.N.S.)—The American corridor being constructed through Canada as part of the International Highway to connect the United States mainland with Alaska looms as the most important project on this continent since the Panama Canal was completed.

STRATEGIC VALUE

Estimates of the cost—twenty-five million dollars—may be greatly exceeded as the work progresses. The United States is paying the costs, with Canada furnishing the land necessary in the dominion route.

The strategic value of the road, in the event Japan attempts to invade Alaska and the Canadian Northwest, is beyond computation in dollars.

Engineers have only a vague idea of the terrain and possible difficulties that are to be met. For much of the distance through the vast Northern Canadian reaches there are no maps, and many of the British Columbia valleys and mountain lands never have been visited by a white man.

READY IN ONE YEAR

It is approximately 1,500 miles from Winnipeg to the end of the railroad in Northern Alberta, 100 miles west of the Peace River. It is approximately 3,000 miles, as the crow flies, from there to Fairbanks, Alaska, northern terminus.

Twists and turns necessary for grades and engineering difficulties will add many, many miles to the distance that the crow flies.

Peacetime estimates of three years for completion of the road will be cut down to a single year by military necessity.

Dollars and manpower will not be conserved in this project. Speed is the watchword.

GREAT WEALTH

Three eight-hour shifts are being provided for, and from the northern end similar activity is being shown.

A fleet of small planes is being used in helping to chart the route and aid in map work.

Aside from its military value—now the uppermost issue—the road will undoubtedly prove an asset of enormous possibilities.

There are known to be in the vast unsurveyed region mineral wealth of untold value, coal deposits that could supply the world's needs for generations, and timber and agricultural resources to support millions.

Margaret Gilbert Honored

BOISE, Idaho, May 2.—Margaret Gilbert of Ada County was elected president of the Idaho County Treasurers' Association at the annual meeting.

Glenn Evans, Shoshone County, was named vice president and Lurine James, Oneida County, secretary. Gracie Pfost, Canyon County; Earl Rice, Idaho County, and Miss Gilbert were named to the legislative committee.

Resolutions were passed opposing tax moratoriums and advocating four-year terms for state and county officials. Present terms are for two years.

Building New Traffic Lane North

JOURNEY'S END — United States Engineer Corps troops arrive at the end of the steel, at Dawson Creek, to start building a highway to Alaska from the end of the present road at Fort St. John's.

IN TROUBLE — First activity of road building at the start of construction of the Alaska Highway. Note men in the foreground with truck pulling another road-building truck out of a ditch. All equipment was shipped from the States for the project.

—(Picture from International News Photograph Service.)

WPB Allows Pump Equipment

CORVALLIS, Ore., May 2.—Farmers of Oregon and other Pacific Coast states who depend on pumping equipment to supply irrigation water for crops have now been assured quotas for such equipment under a revised war production board order which recognizes for the first time that pumping equipment is essential. Notification of this change has just been received by F. E. Price, assistant dean of agriculture at Oregon State College, who spent some time in Washington with other Western representatives urging priorities for irrigation pumping equipment.

Irrigation equipment assigned quotas, ranging from 50 to 132 per cent, include turbine pumps of the smaller sizes and repair parts, centrifugal pumps and repair parts, electric motors for irrigation pumps, and distrbution equipment with repair parts. Some other miscellaneous farm machinery was included in the amended order.

HOTTEST WEATHER

CAIRO, Egypt, May 2.—The hottest weather ever recorded was 136 degrees Fahrenheit at Azizia, Libya, September 13, 1922.

ROUTE TO AIR BASES — Broken line indicates where American engineers hope they will be able to build more than a thousand-mile road along a line of air ports through Canada to Alaska. Dawson Creek will be the southern base for construction supplies, Whitehorse the northern. From Whitehorse, a route is traced to Boundary, north of the Yukon, to Big Delta, where it may link with the highway between Fairbanks and Valdez. Much of the Yukon territory above Whitehorse, however, has never been surveyed.

Palmer Elected by Water Group

HELENA, Mont., May 2.—Election of F. F. Palmer of Forsyth as chairman marked the annual meeting of the Montana section of the American Water Works Association held here. He succeeds H. B. Foote of Helena.

Billings was selected for the 1943 gathering. The association elected S. R. Young of Hardin to succeed Palmer as vice chairman. A. E. Heath of Billings and John Hall of Fort Shaw, trustees, and H. S. Thane of Missoula, director.

WHEAT CROP DROPS

1942 Figures Under 1941

HELENA, Mont., May 2.—More than 26,200,000 bushels of winter wheat will be produced on a million and a quarter acres during 1942, estimates of the bureau of agricultural economics reports.

Although the indicated crop will be about 6 per cent below 1941's top figure of 27,762,000 bushels, it will be more than double the ten-year average of 10,790,000. This year's acreage also will be about 6 per cent below the 1941 total of 1,380,000 acres. A yield of twenty bushels an acre, substantially the same as last year's, is predicted. The ten-year average yield is 11.1 bushels an acre.

Jay Diamond, bureau statistician, said many state farmers this year planted winter wheat in areas which formerly were spring wheat sections. He said that stocks of old wheat on farms included 44 per cent of last year's crop, compared with the previous year's figure at approximately the same time of 37 per cent of the previous year's production.

Desperate to promote the concept of an International Highway from Fairbanks to the lower 48 states, boosters from Fairbanks persuaded Slim Williams and a young companion, John Logan, to ride used custom-built, rigid-framed, lightweight BSA motorcycles cross-country to test the route. The adventurers took seven months to ride the 2,300 miles from Fairbanks to Chicken, Alaska; Dawson and Whitehorse, Yukon; Atlin, Telegraph Creek and Hazelton, British Columbia; to Seattle, Washington. Logan's BSA motorcycle on display at the University of Alaska Museum in Fairbanks. UNIVERSITY OF ALASKA MUSEUM

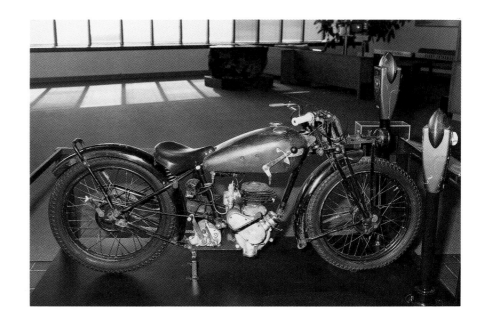

On February 22, 1941, I became an enlisted soldier with the Alaska Communication System (ACS). My first duty was radio operating on the message handling circuits between Alaska and Seattle. A few months later I was assigned to the school for teaching the international morse code to new enlistees in the ACS.

During the month of May 1942, 16 men from the school sent to the Alcan Highway to perform communication duties. There were several other 16-man detachments from other signal corps schools also assigned to areas covering the length of the road to establish communications between all of the company construction crews. Our detachment covered the area between Whitehorse, Yukon, and Fairbanks, Alaska.

I was transferred to Kluane Lake along with two other radio operators. We manned a radio relay link between Whitehorse and Fairbanks. Messages were sent and received between these two locations, plus communications to and from radio-equipped vehicles that were assigned to the construction companies. This activity continued until the ribbon-cutting ceremony upon completion of the highway.

The Kluane Lake location was known as Silver City during the gold-rush days.

Our communication group was a detachment of the 93rd Engineer Battalion. The personnel of the 93rd were Black, except for the officers and Signal Corps men.

— Malcolm G. Parks
Gig Harbor, Washington

More scenes in Silver City, Yukon. MALCOLM PARKS

Lt. Richard L. Newberger,* an aide to Gen. James A. O'Connor, wrote this letter to Alaska Congressman Anthony J. Dimond. Dimond was unable to attend the Nov. 20, 1942 opening ceremony of the Alaska Highway at Soldier's Summit, Yukon.

The letter is chatty, informal and has some little-known details about what went on behind the scenes. It is also poetic, philosophical and contains a rare brand of humor for a military officer.

Dear Tony:

The ceremony opening the Alcan International Military Highway has come and gone and now the road is in actual operation. The first trucks have arrived in Fairbanks. Appropriately enough, the first vehicle ever driven overland from the interior of North America was piloted by a pair of enlisted soldiers, a corporal from Chicago and a private from Minneapolis. This was at the direct order of Gen. O'Connor, who felt that enlisted men should share in this culmination event of the construction of the road.

As delegate in Congress from Alaska, you will be interested in some of the background of the opening ceremony. The most interesting features of any public event always occur in that twilight zone between its evident phases and the part which is wholly preparatory. It was a ceremony international in character. Your friend Bob Bartlett led a representative delegation from Juneau. The Honorable Ian Mackenzie of the Canadian Cabinet headed an outstanding delegation from Ottawa. Gen. Geo. R. Pearkes represented Canada's armed forces. In 1914 Pearkes was a constable in the Royal Mounted at Whitehorse. He told me that some of the territory he drove over en route to the ceremony he once patrolled on horseback in a scarlet tunic. When the first World War broke out Constable Pearkes resigned from the Mounted and enlisted in the Canadian Army. He won the Victoria Cross for valor, and now commands the Pacific Command of his country.

Just as the construction of the highway demonstrated the ingenuity of our soldiers and workers on a large scale, the ceremony opening the highway demonstrated that ingenuity on a much smaller scale.

We had no printing press, yet programs seemed indispensable. What to do? Mimeographing was too colorless and drab. The blueprinting machine of the Public Roads Administration finally was pressed into service. Jean Ewen, PRA design engineer, made some excellent Arctic drawings. Gay Pinkstaff, PRA photographer, ran off the copies. The result was a program which many people thought was not only printed, but actually engraved.

It was quite a task to find distinctive food because supply

difficulties in the wilderness are enormous as you know. We finally relied on Nature's larder. Maj. Dick Luckow sent out hunting parties. The result was moose meat, mountain sheep steaks, and a thinned-out black bear.

We gave all the groceries local names: Dawson Creek Crackers, Fairbanks Cheese, Slims River Salad which turned out to be lettuce and hot-house tomatoes. We never succeeded in convincing any of the guests that the lettuce and tomatoes were picked right outside at 40 degrees below.

Where to hold the ceremony? This problem was a stickler for a month. Finally Col. T.W. Essig made a trip over the road. He selected Soldier's Summit. This is a stretch of highway 1,500 feet above the wide swath of Kluane Lake. Above the road crags tower. Below, the lake is spread out like a vast inland sea. The setting symbolizes the vastness which the highway penetrates.

The participants in the dedication ceremony, accompanied by newspaper correspondents and photographers, drove from Whitehorse to Kluane Lake on a day that crowded 15 below. Many feet tender from the luxuries of civilization, were chilled by the time the new spruce barracks at Kluane were reached. Everyone slept that night dormitory style. The blueprinted programs were given out and privates traded autographs with colonels. A Negro soldier asked Gen. O'Connor for his autograph, and the general climbed out of his sleeping bag, put on his spectacles and signed the soldier's program. "That's the epitome of democracy, isn't it?" Bob Bartlett asked Ian Mackenzie as they watched.

When we went to bed all of us were slightly apprehensive over the fact that neither Gen. Pearkes nor Gen. Ganong of Canada's Eighth Division had arrived. They had been delayed by bad flying weather but were expected later. I think I went to sleep about 10 o'clock. Sometime later I was awakened by a gentle padding on the lumber floor. I cautiously peeked out of a corner of the bag. Gen. O'Connor, in his long underwear, with his fur cap on his head and his parka thrown over his shoulders, was tip-toeing to the door. He threw it open and a lusty "Haloo there!" came through.

The red hat bands and lapels of British general officers appeared in the darkened portal and in walked Gen. Pearkes and Ganong. I lay there in my sleeping bag and struggled between comfort and duty. The bag was warm and comfortable. Yet I was Gen. O'Connor's aide. Could I stay in bed while he welcomed our late-comers? Soon another shape in long underwear emerged. It was Col. K.B. Bush, our chief of staff. He and Gen. O'Connor, looking like union-suit advertisements, were conveying the Canadian generals to their bunks. My conscience overcame my drowsy laziness and I got up and added my size 42 underwear to the scene. "You chaps look quite nifty in there," said Lt. Bob Baile, the aid

*Newberger later became a U.S. senator from Oregon.

to Gen. Pearkes. This was British politeness at its kindest.

In the morning the ceremony was held. It was an event full of color, drama and significance. Col. Bush's hands became blue as he took off his gloves to read the statements received from yourself and many other distinguished men in public life. A long file of Royal Mounties stood at attention in their scarlet coats and leather boots. Their feet must have been as cold as anvils, but they stood as straight and rigid as signal poles. "Discipline and tradition account for that," said Col. Bush. Inspector William Grennan, commanding the Mounties in the Yukon, nodded his assent.

All the speakers stressed the historic importance of what was taking place . . . Ian Mackenzie spoke most eloquently for Canada and brought an inspiring message from Prime Minister King. The ceremony moved towards a natural climax. At its end Mackenzie and Bartlett were given a pair of scissors that had been specially engraved in Alaska gold by William Osborne, pioneer resident of Juneau. The crowd became tense. Then the blades closed and the red, white and blue ribbon across the road was severed. In the cold and gloom of the Arctic morning an American Army band played "God Save the King," then the strains of the "Star Spangled Banner" filled the snowy air.

As the basalt cliffs flung back the last strains of the music a great cheer went up from the crowd. I hurried from Gen. O'Connor's side and struggled to save the ribbon for posterity. The first truck bound for Fairbanks rolled forward as the band played "The Maple Leaf Forever" and "Washington Post."

The general had declared that rank and file soldiers, who did so much to construct the road, were to be given genuine representation at the ceremony. The ribbon was held by four enlisted men . . . two of them Negroes, symbols of the coloured troops whose toil has played a material part in the 1,630-mile undertaking.

After the ceremony lunch was served in the barracks. The smell of spruce pitch and wood grain was still in the air. Boughs hung from the ceiling. The crimson tunics of the Mounties mingled with the somber khaki of their American allies. We ate moose meat and mountain sheep. Cigar and cigarette smoke hung beneath the beams. The band played Johann Strauss' "Tales From Vienna Woods" and the "Blue Danube," lilting memories of a land which may soon be free. It was like some scene from a Graustrakian operetta. Inspector Grennan swayed his head to the gay waltzes, and so did the American mess sergeant who hurried along the tables seeing to it that no one's plate was empty.

It was an episode which will not soon be forgotten by those who participated in it. My own most vivid memory of it is the playing of our national anthem at Soldier's Summit. As the music faded away and I looked around me at the stern faces of the American soldiers and the grim countenances of the Mounties, I felt sure that in such as a scene as this lay the future of the United Nations—that in the ability of us all, Canadians, Americans and Alaskans, white and black, civilian and soldier, to fuse together our efforts in such a project as the Alcan Highway rests the hope of free peoples throughout the earth.

With best wishes, Tony, I am
Your friend,
Dick

The first truck from Dawson Creek, the southern terminus of the road, leads a convoy through Whitehorse 900 miles north to Fairbanks. The trip to Whitehorse took Cpl. Otto Gronke and Pvt. Bob Bowe 72 hours.
YA, SIMMONS COLL. 82/192 #10

Program

Invocation — Father Charles Hamel, O.M.I.
Opening Remarks — Col. K.B. Bush, G.S.C.
Master of Ceremonies
Reading of Messages — Col. John W. Wheeler, C.E.
Introductions
  Col. E.G. Paules - Whitehorse Sector;
  Col. Robert D. Ingalls - Ft. St. John Sector;
  Enlisted Men who will hold the Ribbon:
  Corp. Refines Sims Jr., Pvt. Alfred Jalufka
    Whitehorse Sector;
  Mstr. Sgt. Andrew E. Doyle, Corp. John T. Reilly
    Fort St. John Sector.
Message from the Canadian Armed Forces
  Maj. Gen. George R. Pearkes.
Message from Public Roads Administration
  and Civilian Contractors
  Mr. J.S. Bright, District Engineer.
Message from the Premier of Alberta
  by Hon. W.A. Fallow.
Further Reading of Messages — Col. Bush
Remarks — Dr. Charles Camsell.
  Commissioner Northwest Territories
Introduction of Insp. William Grennan, R.C.M.P.
Speech for Dominion of Canada and Reading of
Message from the Prime Minister by Hon Ian Mackenzie
Speech for Territory of Alaska and Reading of
Message from the Governor by Hon. E.L. Bartlett.
Response on behalf of the American Army,
  Brig. Gen. James A. O'Connor, commanding N.W. Serv. Command
Cutting of Ribbon — Mr. Mackenzie, Mr. Bartlett
"GOD SAVE THE KING" - "THE STAR SPANGLED BANNER"
  U.S. Army Bands
Benediction — Capt. Erwin T. May, Chaplain, U.S.A.

ALASKA·CANADA HIGHWAY

DEDICATION
KLUANE LAKE ~YUKON~
NOVEMBER · 20 TH · 1942·

Menu

SUPPER
Thursday, November 19, 1942, 6 PM

ST. ELIAS MOUNTAIN SHEEP
Nosheep Brown Gravy
Spinach à la Kloo - Takhini Con
Tanana Potatoes
SLIMS RIVER SALAD
Chisana Apple Sauce - Siwash Geldin
Coffee à la Yukon
China-Way Tea
Moose Milk
Sour Dough Bread - Bull-Dozer Butter

BREAKFAST
Friday, November 20, 7:15 AM

Burwash Prunes
Grapefruit Juice - Alcan - Tomato Juice
Alberta Farina
Aishihik Sausage - Dezadeash Eggs
Toast - Butter
Coffee - Sugar - Milk

DINNER
Friday, November 20, 12 Noon

CHAMPAGNE SOUP
MOOSE STEAK à la Donjek
Pickhandle Beans - Kaskawulsh Potatoes
Nabesna Peas and Carrots
KLUANE SALAD
HORSE CAMP PUDDING
Dawson Creek Crackers - Fairbanks Cheese
1630 Miles Coffee
Tea - Orange Juice - Milk
Bread - Butter

COMMITTEE: Col. T.W. Essig, Maj. R.C. Luckom,
Maj. E.N. Stars, Capt. P.L. Reed Co. F.R.R. Johnson,
Lt. F.C. Bishop, Lt. B.B. Miller, Lt. R.J. Neuberger.

E.L. Bartlett reads a message from the governor of the Territory of Alaska. YA

General O'Connor address-ing the crowd. YA

Dignitaries lined up for the ribbon cutting. YA

Father Charles Hamel, O.M.I., reading the invocation. NA

The honorable Ian Mackenzie reading a message on behalf of Prime Minister Mackenzie King of Canada.
YA, SIMMONS COLL. 82/192 #8

Brig. Gen. James O'Connor, left, watches as E.L. "Bob" Bartlett, middle, and Ian Mackenzie cut the ribbon.
YA, SIMMONS COLL. 82/192 #9

The American Guard of
Honor. YA & LC-USW33-932-ZC

Members of the RCMP
Guard of Honor. YA

TRUCKS ROLL NORTH ON ALASKA HIGHWAY

Ceremony in Yukon Wilderness Ends With Cutting of Ribbons to Let Them Pass

OFFICIALS LOOK TO FUTURE

General O'Connor Hails the New Bond Between Alaska, Canada and the U. S.

By THEODORE H. STRAUSS

Special to THE NEW YORK TIMES.

KLUANE LAKE, Yukon Territory, Nov. 21 — The wilderness route to Alaska is open today, seven months and seventeen days after building of the 1,600-mile road began.

In the presence of a small group of Army officers and government officials gathered yesterday on the bleak slopes of Soldier's Summit overlooking the frozen lake below, Ian Mackenzie of the Canadian Cabinet and E. L. Bartlett, Secretary of State of Alaska, cut a red, white and blue ribbon, formally opening the Alcan International Highway.

As the first land link was completed between the United States and its great territory in the north, a thin snow swept down from the St. Elias Range, heaped in lonely grandeur to the west. Despite huge bonfires the 250 witnesses, including Grover Whalen of New York, stamped their feet to keep warm in the sub-zero temperature.

Brig. Gen. James A. O'Connor, commanding the Northwest Service Command, Mr. Mackenzie, Mr. Bartlett and others acclaimed the highway as an epic pioneering achievement significant not only as a present vital military link with the continental bastions of Alaska but also as a future pathway opening a new frontier.

Passage of First Through Truck

The exercises began at 9:30 in the morning just as a gray Arctic dawn was breaking. Colonel K. B. Bush, chief of staff of the Northwest Service Command, was master of ceremonies.

A military band played martial airs and a column of Royal Canadian Mounted Police, led by Inspector William Grennan of Dawson, commanding the Yukon force, lent color to the scene.

As the ribbon was cut, a ton-and-a-half truck, which had made the trip from Dawson Creek, the road's southern terminus, to White Horse in seventy-one hours, led a line of freight trucks past the barrier along the lonely stretch toward Fairbanks.

The first truck to make the complete run was driven by Corporal Otto Gronke of Chicago and Private Bob Bowe of Minneapolis. The muffled applause of gloved hands broke the Arctic silence as they stepped into first gear and moved northward.

Messages of congratulation were read from Vice President Wallace, Governor Ernest Gruening and Delegate Anthony J. Dimond of Alaska, Secretary of War Stimson, Lieut. Gen. Brehon Somervell, Premier William Aberhart of Alberta and Premier John Hart of British Columbia.

Mr. Wallace predicted that the road would be part of an eventual highway serving the New World from Southern South America to Siberia. Governor Gruening urged its extension to the Bering Sea and Mr. Dimond hailed it as a coordination of intelligence, energy and persevering labor.

Many speakers said that the road was a swift route to our Allies in China and Russia.

Sharing of Golden Scissors

The scissors used to cut the ribbon were gold engraved, and Colonel Bush announced that they would be broken apart, with one blade going to President Roosevelt and the other to Prime Minister Mackenzie King.

The absence most marked was that of Brig. Gen. William Hoge, who first began the building of the road from White Horse last Spring and is now on active assignment elsewhere.

General O'Connor, short and stocky, declared in response to the presentation of a service flag from the Alaskan chapter of the Daughters of the American Revolution, that the road was a bond between the United States, Canada and Alaska, and that it had a future significance which no one could now fully estimate.

He praised the all-out spirit of the soldiers and civilians who built the road. In future time, he said, men would tell their children of the building of the road, and as the tales grew taller and taller, it was possible that the Alcan Highway might become an American saga ranking with the epics of Fremont and Lewis and Clark.

Mr. Mackenzie said that Canada had provided the soil while the United States provided the toil.

Major Gen. George R. Pearkes, Chief of the Pacific Command of the Canadian Army, brought greetings from Canada's armed forces. He was accompanied by Major Gen. H. N. Ganong of the Canadian Eighth Division.

The Alcan Highway, built by United States Army engineers and a contingent of civilian workmen, must still be surfaced and its bridges rebuilt to be turned into a permanent structure. A thousand miles of it, from Dawson Creek to Fairbanks, is open and winds through a vast wilderness hardly touched by man. A new frontier has been reached.

Article from the New York Times, *November 22, 1942.*

Mr. Harley Hart trucked on the Alaska Highway in 1942-43. His sweatshirt is now part of the collection in the Fort St. John–North Peace Museum in Fort St. John, B.C.

A Merry Christmas
and
A Happy
New Year
from The Alaska - Canada Highway
Whitehorse - Yukon Territory - Christmas - 1942
· U·S· Public · Roads ·
· Administration ·

SEASON'S GREETINGS

U.S. P.R.A. 1942 ALCAN HIGHWAY

Alaska Highway GREETINGS from Fort St. John B.C. CANADA

The Alaska Highway

VACATION TRIPS on the WHITE PASS AND YUKON ROUTE

Mile marker at the Fort Nelson Heritage Museum, Fort Nelson, B.C. EARL BROWN

Mile marker at MacBride Museum, Whitehorse, Yukon.
WAYNE TOWRISS

One of the few structures left from the wartime construction days is this primitive tower at an abandoned airfield near Pink Mountain, B.C.

GERTRUDE

ED KERRY AND "GERTRUDE", HIS 1938 INTERNATIONAL
TD 35 TRACTOR, CAME TO THE YUKON AS A TEAM
IN THE 1940'S DURING THE BUILDING OF THE ALASKA
HIGHWAY. GERTRUDE'S ACCOMPLISHMENTS SPANNED 40
YEARS, AND INCLUDE CONSTRUCTION OF AIRSTRIPS, CITY
STREETS IN WHITEHORSE, PORTIONS OF THE ALASKA
HIGHWAY, AND CONSTRUCTION SITES ALL OVER THE YUKON.
"GERTIE" WAS DONATED TO THE YUKON GOVERNMENT BY
THE KERRY FAMILY IN MEMORY OF ED KERRY, A LOYAL
AND TRUE YUKONER.

Tractor on display at the Watson Lake Highway Interpretive Center.

A 1936 D-8 Cat and other original construction equipment are on display at the Fort Nelson Heritage Museum, Fort Nelson, B.C. DALE JENKINS & EARL BROWN

This monument is located at Mile 757.9/1261 km, near the Morley River Lodge, Yukon.

During the 1992 50th Anniversary year, historical signs were placed along the highway in British Columbia, the Yukon and Alaska to tell the story of the construction years, 1942-44.

A new bridge has been placed at the site of Contact Creek, B.C.

50th Anniversary Display on The Alaska Highway at the University of Alaska Museum, Fairbanks.

Typical tire shop artifacts as used on the highway.

Display of artifacts used by the U.S. Army on the highway: officer's wool tunic, soldier's sewing kit, musette bag, baking stone, cigarettes, canvas shelter, wool blanket, aerial survey camera.

30

Typical roadhouse artifacts.

Artifacts used by the civilian contractors.

In July 1992 a fire completely destroyed the Sikanni Chief Bridge near mile 159, km 256, on the Alaska Highway. Arson is suspected. The bridge, completed in the 1943 reconstruction of the highway, was one of the last PRA bridges left on the road. Although it was bypassed years ago, it was still in good usable condition.
SIKANNI RIVER LODGE
& RIVER PARK

This Ford-made jeep (1942) completed a round-trip on the Alaska Highway during July and August 1992 to celebrate the 50th anniversary of the completion of the pioneer road. Owned by Fred LaPerriere of Denver, Colo., it is one of 1,500 produced with the Ford's name stamped on it. The jeep was rescued from a mining operation in southern Colorado and was completely restored to its 1942 condition. Along with LaPerriere were his uncle Bob LaPerriere, John Cronhart and Bob Bowman.

Pictures from Dawson Creek's Opening Ceremonies Held Feb. 15-16, 1992

Open Air Ceremony held in front of the Mile Zero Post in Dawson Creek on Sunday, Feb. 16, 1992. The ceremony marked the official opening of the 50th Anniversary and the start of the Snowmobile Safari, the first cross jurisdictional event to be held in 1992.

On Saturday, Feb. 15, 1992, an indoor event was held in the Dawson Creek Arena. The arena was transformed into a performing theater. Local talent was very much in evidence as well as international stars, such as Joelle Rabu, Frank Gorshin, George Fox and Colin James. Leslie Nielsen was appointed Grand Marshall of the Alaska Highway at this event. Shown here are local entertainears "Northern Lights Jazz Choir" performing favorite hits from the 1940s.

Frank Gorshin, famous impressionist; Joelle Rabu, singer; and local entertainers "The Silhouettes," pose in front of the Mile Zero Post in a circa-1942 Jeep.

DAWSON CREEK RENDEZVOUS 92
COMMUNITY COMMITTEE VIA ELLEN COREA

The original site of the Soldier's Summit dedication ceremony on the Alaska Highway at Mile 1029, km 1707, above Kluane Lake has been established as a memorial. A re-enactment of the Nov. 20, 1942, ceremony was performed on Nov. 20, 1992. The original flagpoles have been replaced, but more than 50 years later they are still lying on the ground in a decayed condition.

About 150 men and women braved minus 21 degree temperatures on Nov. 20, 1992, for the re-dedication of Soldier's Summit at Kluane Lake, Yukon. The re-enactment of the ribbon-cutting ceremony featured original speeches from the 1942 event which was attended by Canadian and American military and government dignitaries. WHITEHORSE STAR

Yukon Commissioner Ken McKinnon gives his speech at the ceremony. YUKON ANNIVERSARIES COMMISSION

A contingent of RCMP personnel attended the ceremony. YUKON ANNIVERSARIES COMMISSION

Invited guests sat down to a moose steak dinner in a tent on the Slims River Flats following the re-enactment ceremonies. YUKON ANNIVERSARY COMMISSION

The Alaska Highway
La route de l'Alaska
1942-1992

42
CANADA

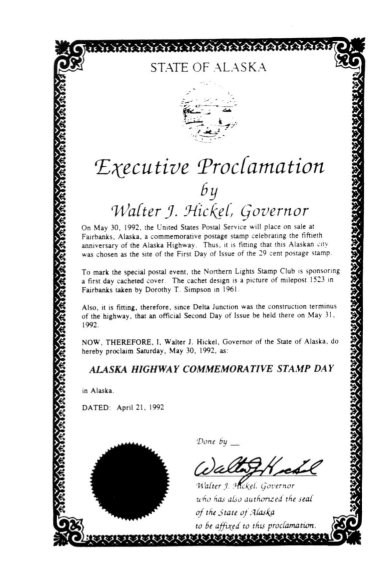

STATE OF ALASKA

Executive Proclamation
by
Walter J. Hickel, Governor

On May 30, 1992, the United States Postal Service will place on sale at Fairbanks, Alaska, a commemorative postage stamp celebrating the fiftieth anniversary of the Alaska Highway. Thus, it is fitting that this Alaskan city was chosen as the site of the First Day of Issue of the 29 cent postage stamp.

To mark the special postal event, the Northern Lights Stamp Club is sponsoring a first day cacheted cover. The cachet design is a picture of milepost 1523 in Fairbanks taken by Dorothy T. Simpson in 1961.

Also, it is fitting, therefore, since Delta Junction was the construction terminus of the highway, that an official Second Day of Issue be held there on May 31, 1992.

NOW, THEREFORE, I, Walter J. Hickel, Governor of the State of Alaska, do hereby proclaim Saturday, May 30, 1992, as:

ALASKA HIGHWAY COMMEMORATIVE STAMP DAY

in Alaska.

DATED: April 21, 1992

Done by __

Walter J. Hickel, Governor
who has also authorized the seal
of the State of Alaska
to be affixed to this proclamation.

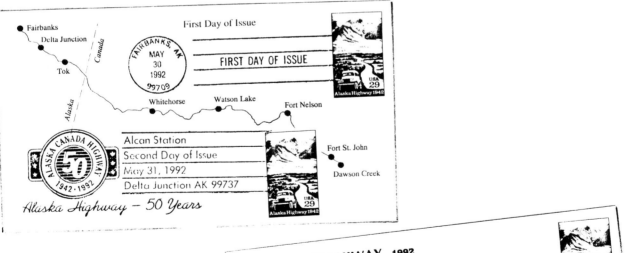

CHAPTER THREE

THE CANOL PROJECT

A workman stands at an oil-soaked station on the Canol pipeline near Norman Wells, N.W.T. Imperial Oil Company of Canada produced the oil at Norman Wells while the Standard Oil Company of California operated the pipeline and refinery at Whitehorse.

Miles and miles of pipe for the pipeline were assembled at this camp near Whitehorse.

Unloading 23-foot sections of pipe to be placed on barges for the trip downriver to Canol Camp.

At a Canol camp, 23-foot lengths of pipe in the foreground were welded into 45-foot lengths which were stored in the background, ready for loading onto trucks. Welders produced 25 joints an hour.

A common sight along the Canol road during the construction days.

Sections of pipe were loaded on the White Pass and Yukon Railroad at Skagway and brought north to the Whitehorse area.

The Canol road and pipeline traversed through Dodo Canyon on its way to Canol Camp and Norman Wells.

Two workmen boil a pot of water over a small campfire next to their equipment in Dodo Canyon.

Black troops try to pull out a truck stuck on the Canol road.

A Canol camp somewhere in the Yukon. Camps such as this were home to thousands of Canadian and American military and civilian construction workers.

A Canol worker stands in the doorway of a "wannigan," an uninsulated shack that was home to thousands of construction workers. The initials BPC stood for Bechtel, Price, Callaghan, a consortium of three American companies formed in 1942 to build the road and pipeline.

Father Maurice Beauregard, O.M.I., head of the Roman Catholic mission at a Canol camp, was also an expert at watch repairs. In his spare time he was kept busy repairing watches for the construction workers along the road and pipeline project.

Two U.S. Army officers stand up to their ankles in mud, surveying a portion of the Canol road in Dodo Canyon.

Interior and exterior remains of U.S. Army Quonset huts along the Canol Road and a warehouse at Camp Canol. All these structures have now been demolished. NORMAN WELLS HISTORICAL CENTER

The Canol pipeline, road and telephone line originally went through Dodo Canyon. Little trace now remains due to severe spring flooding. The Mile 36 pumping station was originally located in the lower right-hand corner of the photo. This view is looking east toward Norman Wells. NORMAN WELLS HISTORICAL SOCIETY

Hunters on the Canol Road at Milepost 79.

White Pass & Yukon railroad facilities at the north end of Skagway, 1944. NA 208-LU-S-Q-1

CHAPTER FOUR

TRANSPORTATION SYSTEMS

Headquarters and Supply Company of the 770th Railway Operating Battalion of the U.S. Army Transportation Corps in Skagway. YA, PRESTON COLL.

More personnel of the 770th at the Skagway roundhouse. YA, PRESTON COLL.

770th personnel at Whitehorse. YA, PRESTON COLL.

This steel cantilever bridge over Dead Horse Gulch was built in the early 1900s and was still in use during the war. It has now been bypassed by a small bridge and tunnel.
MALCOLM PARKS

Skagway was a busy railroad town in this 1944 view. The railroad operated day and night to supply the Alaska Highway and Canol Pipeline construction projects in the Yukon.
NA 208-LU-4-Z-2

Army Transportation Service riverboats at Bethel (left) and McGarth (right). Riverboats provided a valuable service during the war, hauling bulk cargo to many sites along Alaska's rivers. KANSAS STATE HISTORICAL SOCIETY

The dock area at Nenana on the Tanana River. Here cargo was transferred from the Alaska Railroad to river barges for trans-shipment to towns and airfields down the Tanana River to the Yukon River. KANSAS STATE HISTORICAL SOCIETY

A raft on the Tanana River that carried 55-gallon fuel drums to sites on the Yukon River. KANSAS STATE HISTORICAL SOCIETY

Unloading facilities at Galena on the Yukon River, site of an auxiliary airfield for the Russian Lend-Lease program. KANSAS STATE HISTORICAL SOCIETY

Many small sternwheelers such as this were used on the inland waters of northern Alberta and the Northwest Territories to transport equipment and supplies for the Canol Pipeline project. LC-USW33-931-ZC

Carcross, Yukon, was a major trans-shipment point for the Canol Pipeline project. Supplies were brought here by the White Pass & Yukon Railroad and then sent by truck to Johnson's Crossing on the Alaska Highway, the starting point for the Canol Road. Carcross is at the northern end of Lake Bennett, a major stern-wheeler center for a series of lakes in the Yukon and northern British Columbia. The large boat, the *Tutshi*, pictured, plied the lakes for years until it was beached and turned into a tourist attraction. Unfortunately the boat burned to the ground in 1990. The old engine, Duchess, is still on display at Carcross. YA, PEPPER COLL.

The last remaining stern-wheelers still in use on the Yukon River, the *Klondike*, the *Keno* and the *Casca* were extensively used during the war years to carry supplies downriver to towns in the Yukon River—the *Klondike*, the *Keno* and the *Casca*—were the *Keno* is displayed at Dawson City. The era of the riverboats came to an end in 1955. TOP: NA 208-LU-4-Y-7, MIDDLE & BOTTOM: YA, PEPPER COLL.

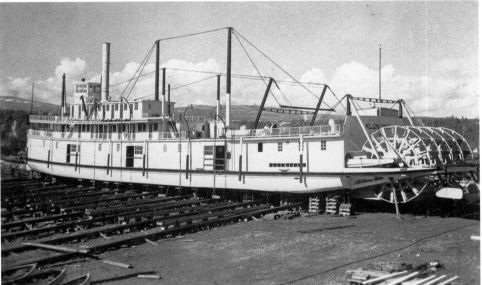

The *Casca*, docked on
the Yukon River.
NA 208-LU-24-G-3

The *Keno* at Teslin, Yukon, in
1942. YA, PEPPER COLL.

Pipe for the Canol project
was loaded on barges from
the railroad at Whitehorse for
trans-shipment to other
points. YA, PRESTON COLL.

CHAPTER FIVE

COMMUNICATIONS & RUSSIAN LEND-LEASE

FORM No. S. C. 144-A.

Signal Corps United States Army
ALASKA COMMUNICATION SYSTEM
TELEGRAM

Pay Nothing Unless Written in Ink on Delivery Sheet.

ALASKA S.S.C.
MAY 20 1942
SEWARD

NUMBER

CHARGES

forward to Anchorage

U.S. Army Signal Corps telegraph delivery men stand ready in front of the Signal Corps office in the Federal Building, downtown Anchorage. From 1900 to 1970, when the Alaska Communication System was sold to a private firm, the military provided all long-line communication services in Alaska. USA

Army Airways Communications System in the Aleutian campaign

By Robert J. Gleason

Not quite ready

When the Japanese struck, Alaska was not at all prepared for war in the air although some preparation had begun as early as 1939. Ladd Field had been built at Fairbanks and when war came Elmendorf Field at Anchorage was nearing completion. The Navy had constructed air bases at Sitka and Kodiak and a base was under construction at Dutch Harbor in the Aleutians. Pan American Airways, during the 1930s, had built a chain of aeronautical radio-telegraph stations from Seattle through British Columbia into Fairbanks, Nome and Bethel and these facilities were all in operation and ready to serve. The CAA (now FAA) did not come into Alaska to build any airports or facilities until 1939. As the war began, contractors were hard at work on many fields, communication stations, and radio aids to navigation on the Alaska Peninsula, with one exception. Very secretly, a U.S. Army Air Force field had been built by Army engineers on Umnak Island, some 60 miles from Dutch Harbor.

Before Pearl Harbor AACS had only small detachments at Ladd and Elmendorf Fields but the 11th and 16th Communication Regions had been activated and by the spring of 1942 there were several AACS stations in operation from Annette Island (near Ketchikan) to Cold Bay and from Montana through Canada into Fairbanks and on to Nome. In addition to serving the 11th Air Force, which was opposing the Japanese thrust, AACS was deeply engaged in serving the Air Transport Command and the Naval Air Transport Service on the routes to Alaska up the Pacific coast and also through Canada.

There were many serious coordination problems with weather codes, cryptographic codes, message formats, frequencies and circuitry to be agreed upon and put into use by USAAF, Royal Canadian Air Force, Navy, Canadian Department of Transport and the CAA. At the foundation of these agreements were the Joint American-Canadian Agreement and the Presidential Order. By the fall of 1942 operational plans and circuitry were pretty well settled.

Source of supply

Of course the big problem of equipment was always at the head of everyone's list. The Alaska Communication System of the Signal Corps was the AACS source of supply for Alaska and was doing a mighty job of coping with all the demands on them with communications and radio navigation equipment in short supply throughout the world.

Virtually all aircraft operation in Alaska was on visual flight rules, though some instrument operation had begun using the few range stations that had been built.

As the first step in containing the Japanese, U.S. Navy and Army forces moved onto unoccupied Adak Island on Aug. 30, 1942. By ingeniously damming and draining a tidal lagoon, U.S. Army engineers were able to provide a useable air strip in only two weeks. This put our aircraft 385 miles closer to Kiska—now only 265 miles away. AACS moved in immediately with a rudimentary control tower and air/ground and point-to-point facilities linking the new field to Umnak and other stations to the east.

As the field on Adak was improved and fighter and bomber aircraft based there, the Japanese air attacks from Kiska using Rufes (Zeros on floats) were gradually stopped. The Japanese were prevented from completing an airfield on Kiska and their aircraft were destroyed in the air or on the beaches. Their shipping was also continually harrassed and some ships sunk.

The weather was the primary enemy of all air operations with fog, low clouds, high winds and rain conditions almost unending. The weather helped the Japanese and was a constant danger for our pilots. Forecasting Aleutian weather is extremely difficult most of the time and our operational losses were heavy—many times aircraft were unable to return to bases because the weather closed in quickly. To help prevent such losses, AACS provided a number of weather reporting stations on outlying islands, some of which were established with great difficulty.

Navigational aids

With the assistance of two CAA engineers, a loop range was installed on Umnak and helped greatly in instrument let-downs to the field, which had clear approaches. Regular instrument operation was begun by the Troop Carrier Squadron with its C-47s. Adak approaches were far more difficult because of the mountainous terrain on Adak and on Great Sitkin Island, but radio aids to navigation were also being installed as rapidly as possible.

The next step out the Aleutian Chain was to install a field on Amchitka Island. U.S. forces moved onto Amchitka on Jan. 12, 1943, and Colonel Talley and his engineers had a useable strip ready on January 28. Amchitka is only 85 miles from Kiska and only 275 from Attu, so the enemy could be readily bombed whenever the weather permitted.

Then came the big decision by our top planners: to remove the Japanese from Attu, bypass and cutoff Kiska, which would be retaken later. On May 11, 1943, U.S. forces landed on Attu on two widely separated beaches. About 2,500 Japanese resisted fiercely to the end. Five hundred and forty-nine Americans were killed and the terrain, cold, snow and rain contributed to another 1,200 American casualties.

With Attu secured on May 30, the engineers again quickly improvised a field and our first aircraft landed on Attu on June 8. Again AACS was there.

Our forces quickly moved onto Shemya Island, a very small but almost flat island, 33 miles from Attu and 190 miles from Kiska. The first aircraft landed on Shemya on June 20.

Plans were now made to remove the Japanese from Kiska. All the routes to Alaska, across Alaska and out the peninsula and the Aleutian Chain were becoming much smoother. AACS was of course involved everywhere, with new men and equipment moving up from the "Lower 48."

Embarrassingly, when U.S. forces moved onto Kiska on Aug. 15, 1943, it was found that under cover of fog the Japanese Navy had sneaked in and evacuated every Japanese.

Thus ended the Aleutian Campaign. After this there were some raids run to the Kurile Islands but again, largely because of the weather, U.S. efforts were concentrated in the south and central Pacific. The Japanese in the north had been contained and eliminated.

It is 1,720 miles from Anchorage to Attu—a long and rugged airway. All the men of AACS who slugged it out through wind, rain, sleet and mud to maintain this service can be very proud.

Robert J. Gleason began his career in communications in 1926, alternating between college and working as a radio operator on ships and at salmon cannery stations in Alaska. He earned a bachelor of science in electrical engineering in 1931 at the University of Washington and a year later was hired by Pan American World Airways to begin building an aeronautical radio-telegraph system across Alaska. He joined the Army Airways Communication System in 1942 and served in key assignments in Alaska, the China-Burma-India Theater, and the North Atlantic. Following World War II he returned to civilian life and retired in 1972. He now lives in Annapolis, Maryland.

Bob Coonrad's remembrances of his time in Alaska with the U.S. Army Communication System

Prior to the posting of the Naval Intelligence notice in mid-May 1942, several things of note happened to break the monotony of the day-to-day existence on Umnak. The first event is one that I am not too proud of; however, the months following Pearl Harbor had everyone a bit jumpy. One day at the ACS station, Sergeant Wheeler noticed some strange objects in motion south of Umnak over the ocean and called this to the attention of several of us. We went out of the radio shack and began to give our total support in viewing this unusual sight. The total number of objects were 12 and they were all in line. The consensus was that if we were ever to see carrier launched aircraft it would be difficult to say anything else than what we were seeing. Sergeant Wheeler went into the shack and immediately alerted the ACS net, indicating that one person in attendance was a member of the Army Air Corps and felt that this lent some credence to the report. Not too long after this someone produced a pair of binoculars and we were then able to discern that these UFOs had wings in motion and were truly nothing more than a flight of the largest black ravens in the world, and indigenous to the Aleutians. This was our first but not last sighting of these birds; however, since this report put all of the ADC on alert status, I, for one, felt very stupid and sheepish. I recall that we were interviewed at some length not long afterwards by various Naval and Army officers to ascertain where we were coming from—whose side were we on, that type of thing.

Also during this time we were given a private show of some of our naval power deployed in the chain. A group of us happened to be looking eastward toward Chernofsky Harbor on Unalaska and observing some of the barges that were nearing Otter Point, and we also were impressed by the rift in the ocean's surface that produced a very noticeable wave-type crest of somewhat stationary condition and of several feet in height that ran almost in a straight line between the two islands. We deduced on our own that this was probably due primarily to the temperature differential between the waters of the Bering Sea and the Pacific Ocean.

While watching barges one day a group of us were much surprised to see steaming from north to south through the Umnak Pass the destroyer USS *Fox;* and the cruisers, USS *Charleston* and USS *Salt Lake City,* all apparently being committed to cruising the south side of the chain in a westward direction. We waved but doubted we could be seen from that distance.

The location of the ACS radio shack also afforded

a very good view of Ship Rock, aptly named as it was shaped exactly like the pirate ships that used to ply the Bounding Main and the port side was exposed to Otter Point. The distance was about one-half mile away from our viewing point. This creation of nature was to play a significant part in the events that followed.

The end of the month of May saw an increase in the number of aircraft arriving at Umnak and as I recall we were working them in on voice and CW communications. This was the first time that we began to have knowledge of the number of revetments that had been under construction. I do not remember that radio silence was imposed on either the AACS or ACS, but, believe this was related to the Navy in the chain. I also believe WYSH, our AACS station at Cold Bay, had been activated by this time and JV and JT were in contact at various times.

June 3 came upon us weather-wise as most days there, misty and blustery, with a solid overcast between 500 to 1,000 feet. It was about noon that we heard two P-40s pass quite low over the ACS radio shack, headed toward the southern end of Ship Rock—many of us ran out the door to see what was happening. It became apparent that a strange aircraft had entered the pass from the south and as it approached the south end of the rock, we could make out the "Red Ball" rising sun marking on the fuselage. The P-40s had made a wide bank to the left and were soon on the tail of the "Pete"; all three soon passed behind Ship Rock headed in a northerly path. Soon thereafter the two P-40s came into view with no "Pete" in sight, so our small group could guess that a member of the Japanese fleet had made the sacrifice to his Emperor, and we shouted and hailed the noble deed. Our ships turned to the south and, as we were to learn later, engaged several more of the observation planes and sent one more into the ocean.

The thought also came rapidly to our minds that the first craft may have had time to radio back to the cruiser or carrier that he had located enemy aircraft at the east end of Umnak. Apparently the enemy didn't relate Umnak with the aircraft they had encountered, thereby allowing us to continue being a secret base for a brief period longer. Things at the ACS building had become somewhat crowded and they needed room, so the two weather buddies, and JV and I, spent time working on the new Quonsets in preparation for moving as soon as practicable.

June 4 appeared with the same lousy weather. I was in the radio shack when the S29 receiver guarding the air to ground frequency of 4495 became active at about 3 p.m. with a voice in English giving directions as to what flights would take various targets—the targets being designated in our service phonetics at the time—i.e. Adam, Baker, Cast, Dog, Easy, Fox, Hypo and Item.

ACS Private Beauchamp also was listening, and soon afterward, Sergeant Wheeler reported to all of us that Dutch Harbor was being bombed by the Japanese.

Immediately after, 4495kc became very busy with mixed voices—one in particular I remember well saying, "O.K. Yank you are cold turkey now." We later heard that Zeros and P-40s got into several dog fights off Unalaska.

Not too long after this we had dog fights going on at the east end of Umnak with some of our newly emplaced GM 40mm "Bofor" type guns throwing "ack-ack" up and smoking the air above us. Jack and I picked up our helmets, rifles, ammo and gas masks and headed for our designated fox holes located next to our new Quonset quarters. As we arrived we looked down to the south and watched bullets ricocheting off the metal runway with many sparks due to friction and tracer trails—many of these whistled over our heads. In a brief moment it became aware where all of this was coming from, for a P-40 loomed with all guns on and no one in front of him. On his tail was a Zero, guns full on, and on his tail another P-40, with his guns on.

Watching the three crafts zoom overhead and all make an abrupt vertical climb into the low overcast sky brought to my mind the old modismo expression had learned in my high school Spanish class, "Poder al lo cielo," or, "make for the ceiling."

This was the baptism by fire for many of our fighter pilots and bomber crews at this time. One has to remember they were pitted against some of the best trained pilots that the enemy had to offer at that time.

The action of our P-40s and Zeros overhead darting in and out of the overcast seemed to last an eternity. It was apparent that the maneuverability of the Zero was far superior to our heavier and better protected P-40. The "ack-ack" carried on through the entire event. This display was probably completed in less than 20 minutes, real time.

I returned to the ACS station and recall receiving a call on 4595kc CW from one of our bombers on patrol to the effect that he had located the Japanese force and was going in for attack; I believe his signature was "Marks." I recall also receiving in the blind a similar message on this frequency from "Freerks," a PBY pilot. All details were logged and JV contacted the Base Operations by signal corps land-line phones with this information.

On June 5 we immediately started the entire AACS station move to our Quonset huts. The weather guys were all moved by this time and lent a hand to our efforts. JV and Curley soon had the Kohler unit going and I concentrated on setting up the transmitter and receivers in the north end of the building. We had been eating only C rations at this time and I became very ill with fever and cough. I tried the mile-walk to the new mess facility and back, but finally hit my bunk in a cold sweat. I believe it was Captain Davis who finally said, "This soldier is going to the hospital as he is on the brink of pneumonia." Fortunately the hospital was no longer a tent, but also a very comfortable Quonset hut, about one-half mile to the north of our new home.

I was rapidly introduced to the latest therapy consisting of Sulfa pills the size of horse tablets. After about five days a Major Moore, M.D., stated that I was out of danger and no further rales were detected. During my stay I will be forever in debt to the Major who was a chaplain and one day produced my S29 Skytraveler receiver so that the few of us in the hospital plus medics could listen to KGEI at night and enjoy the Jack Benny Show, Fibber McGee and others, with Chet Huntley and the news.

Upon return to duty we were very busy with weather and aircraft reports with WYSH, Cold Bay and WZX, Elmendorf Field.

It was late in July that we received our BC401, Collins, Autotune, 400 watt Transmitter. And it was about this time that the CAA personnel came to set up the radio range/adcock system. JV and I were the only AACS operators until late August when Sgts. William Thomas and James Shiner joined our group. The weather people had received a 2nd Lt. Frank Morris, who was a graduate forecaster and was to become our censor for mail purposes. Also, six other weather enlisted personnel appeared at this time.

The new transmitter was installed at a new site several miles to the west of our location. A large swampy area with a board walk was our closest approach. M/Sgt. Louie Felton and one other man-made the installation.

Over and above the sad news about the loss of life at Dutch Harbor some levity did come to light about our attack at Umnak. The following day, June 5, I happened to talk to one of the Jeep drivers on the base and he had been assigned to drive Maj. John Gilkes around the base on June 4. The good major, who had been my squadron commander while I was in the 24th AB Squadron, was for some reason on Umnak at this time and carried a .45 Cal Thompson (Old Round Magazine-Chicago Piano type) machine gun wherever he went. With all of the aerial activity on the 4th he bailed out, according to his driver, and started firing skyward at all and sundry. A few rounds from above hit the tundra near them—the Major took a dive under the Jeep. But Major Gilkes was a fairly large-framed man and he became stuck between the underside of the jeep and the tundra. The driver said it was no mean task to extricate him from his predicament.

One of the pilots of a C-47, Lt. Willie Setzer, who had recently arrived at Umnak prior to the attack, was near his aircraft parked in one of the revetments when the activity took place overhead. His urgent response was to seek shelter behind any large object—his choice as he learned later was not the best—a 500-pound bomb stored at the edge of the area; however, he was lucky and nothing happened. Willie later gained some matter of infamy, as he was the pilot charged with transporting the Bob Hope show down the chain to Umnak and back, later on in 1942. As I recall they hit bad weather near Naknek on the return to Elmendorf and he had his crew chief breakout the chest-type parachutes to the passengers. Needless to say stuff hit the fan over this scare tactic.

I also spoke with the young gun handler on the GM 40mm the next day. He had some sweet words to say about the ordnance sergeant and the civilian GM engineer who strapped him into the gun belt position, loaded him up with a clip and then immediately retreated to the rear of the dugout as things got hot with enemy gunfire all around. He said he got in a few bursts and got into some loading trouble—all his illustrious leaders would say was "Stay in there Kid, you're doing a great job!!"—all the while cringing back out of harm's way with no effort to aid him.

Back to a more serious note: a P-38, one of the first that we had seen, tried to make a takeoff from the landing strip on a northern heading and crashed about one-quarter-mile to the north of us. He wiped out the entire supply of quartermaster flour used to make our bread on the island. The poor pilot paid with his life—not a pleasant sight to behold during the cleanup with which several of us helped.

Meanwhile, the focus of the war moved to the west with the advent of the Japanese occupation of Kiska and Attu. I believe it was in September 1942 that Joe Veliz was sent to Adak and T/Sgt. Joe Lugo was appointed Non-Com In Charge at WYSI, Umnak. Numerous other stations were soon to come on line such as WYSK, Kodiak; WYSD, Naknek; WYSM, Ft. Morrow, and WYSC, Cordova. We, on occasion, would exchange a quick hello with some of our friends at the other stations. An AACS old-timer, M/Sgt. Wilber Stein, was to become Station Chief at WYSH. He had been endowed with the additional duties of monitoring the Net for proper operating discipline and security. The discrepancies were reported on a periodic basis and I was lucky one time to make his "hit parade" for having sent "Dit-Dit" after a transmission. My personal sign was "CD," so there was no mistaking the accuracy of the report.

The greatest thing was we finally got a barn-type shower house late in the fall of '42—only one mile away. This was great during the winter and we would get our pores all opened up and into clean cloths for a journey back to our quarters in sometimes freezing weather.

About February 1943, we moved a mile to the northwest to a new receiving station location with new bays to hold about eight new Hammarlund HQ-120 Receivers complete with new metal desk-type operating position and switching panel for selecting the various receiver outputs. Our living quarters were near and became a hazard to those who did not know where the foxholes were after a good Aleutian snowstorm. We lost one first lieutenant three times in one night—much to Joe Lugo's delight. Joe Lugo, as I recall, returned to Elmendorf soon afterwards and I remained as Chief Operator with the tower NCO in charge (M/Sergeant Cresap).

I remained to get about six newly arrived operators acquainted with their new station and had the fun of getting them to move on building a new Quonset hut quarters—no easy task as for the most part these guys put *Mutiny on the Bounty* in Sunday School category.

It was a very happy day when I went aboard a C-47 bound for Elmendorf on May 9, 1943—yes!! My 21st birthday.

I did make T/Sergeant in July 1943 and stayed at WZX as a high speed operator until I had a run-in with First Sergeant John Mazar (a former Minneapolis policeman)—after a squadron dress down, I was punished by being shipped via the Alaska Railroad to Fairbanks. It was a tremendous experience as we stayed at the Curry Rail Station at mid-point of the journey—which had the best food in Alaska, as they had to cater to the civilian workers who demanded the very best. Also the rail travel along the base of Mt. McKinley, with the view of all the mountain goats and sheep on the craggy slopes above, was awesome. We arrived at the rail station at Fairbanks with the first flakes of snow coming down—Sept. 17, 1943.

I finished my stay in the north at Ladd Field working various CW circuits and the Russki Ops on their way to Nome, Anadyr and points to the eastern front.

I was reassigned to the states departing Ladd on March 13 and arriving on March 21, 1944, at Great Falls, Montana, via Edmonton, Alberta, McChord Field then back to WXEN, Great Falls Air Base. On Jan. 6, 1945, I married WXEN secretary, Mary Louise Davis, a native of Great Falls. I was discharged from Fort Douglas, Utah on May 21, 1945—the same place it all started.

A typical Alaska Communication System office and quarters. This one was located at Flat in the interior of Alaska. At the outbreak of the war, the Army had two Signal Corps companies in the territory. Its personnel were located in the widely scattered and remote communities throughout Alaska. USA

Notes from Stacy H. Dobrzensky, Oakland, California, on Russian Lend–Lease

I served as a Detachment Commander, later as the Squadron Commander, in what began as the 16th Army Airways Communications System Area and became the 60th Group of the 3rd Wing of the Army Airways Communications System. I was originally assigned to Whitehorse, Yukon Territory, reporting in on July 22, 1942. After a year I was transferred to Prince George, British Columbia, then, a year later, to Ladd Field, in Fairbanks, Alaska. After somewhat over a year I was assigned to Edmonton, Alberta. My assignment in Fairbanks was as C.O. of the 123rd AACS Squadron at the time it was established with that designation. My assignment in Edmonton was as C.O. of the 122nd AACS Squadron. I returned to the U.S. after about four months in Edmonton, which was in January of 1946.

★ ★ ★

One of Colonel Vasin's pilots, soloing a P-47, called in to report nose wheel problems when he attempted to land. Colonel Vasin went to our Control Tower (where we had a Russian-speaking operator) and talked the young pilot in. The pilot was frightened and excited, but the colonel's voice, although he spoke in Russian, was soothing and calming. He guided the pilot out over the Cold Weather Test Detachment winter bomb range, had him jettison his underbody extra fuel tank, then circle over a large radius, but in sight of the field, to use up gasoline, ultimately had him head in to land. Our Russian operator gave us a running translation. The Colonel went through all the steps preparatory to land, had him come in fairly fast with his nose high, then try the nosewheel carefully (with enough speed on to take off again). The nosewheel held, the fellow pilots rushed onto the field, got the pilot, left the plane on the runway and carried him back to the main hangar on their shoulders.

★ ★ ★

All of the Base Squadron personnel involved directly in the receipt of ALSIB aircraft and the necessary checks and turning of them over to the Russians, who were great admirers of their favorite flyer— Colonel Vasin. When he was to test-fly a B-25, or one of the other multi-engine planes, he would invite members of the enlisted ground crew to "go for a ride." Generally, the "brass," Tech and Master Sergeants were the lucky ones. On one occasion, in a B-25, he encountered a nose wheel problem himself. This time the tower operators (speaking through the U.S., Russian-speaking operator) observed that the nose wheel was clearly not locked, since it could be seen moving back and forth in the slipstream. The colonel ordered his passengers to crowd to the rear plane so that it flew in a nose-up attitude by reason of the extra rearward weight (B-25 landings were normally nose-up to avoid having the nose wheel hit the ground first.). When he made his landing (after we had alerted the fire and "meat wagon" crews) the aircraft appeared to be in a normal landing "flare"—except that he made a three-point landing on the main wheels and the tail skid (a piece of metal perhaps a foot long, 3-4" wide and an inch or so thick, as protection if the tail should get too low in a landing), keeping as much weight off the skid as he could. The landing was accompanied by a shower of sparks from the rear

skid and ended up with the nose high and the plane resting on the two main wheels and what was left of the skid. As his passengers started to tumble out, Colonel Vasin popped the emergency hatch over his head and yelled at the passengers to get back in! Then, after a tall jack had been produced and the nose stabilized in its "up-in-the-air" attitude, he released his passengers as the ground crew jacked the nose down until it could be rested on a dolly and the plane towed into the hangar!

★ ★ ★

When Vice President Wallace stopped off on his return from his tour of Russia (distributing and gathering seeds, among other things) Colonel Keillor, the Ladd Field Commanding Officer, arranged a joint Russian-American banquet for the Vice President and his party. As a Squadron Commander (123d AACS), I was privileged to attend. There were toasts and speeches (we toasted President Roosevelt and Marshal Stalin and heard from the two colonels (Vasin and Keillor) and a speech and some film from the Vice President. At the table where I was seated was the Vice President's State Department aide, who tore out most of his hair as the Vice President's speech went on—his only comment to his table mates was "he never says what we tell him to say, always says what we tell him not to say!" In the course of the speeches and film of the trip, it was abundantly clear that the Vice President (very wisely) always took along volleyballs and nets, so that he had a means of getting some exercise after the long hours of flying in a C-54, and the many banquets and toasts.

After dinner, Mr. Wallace issued, on behalf of an American team, a challenge at volleyball with a Russian team. Colonel Keillor instructed Lt. Regitko, the Base Athletic Officer, to station him by the exit door and pick an American team. Notwithstanding that Colonel Keillor had just been hospitalized for and was still suffering from a back problem, the Vice President ordered him to play on our team. Being 6'1½", the lieutenant latched onto me and others who were tall, without any regard to skill at volleyball. In short, we played three games, 19-2, 20-1 and 21-0, all in favor of the gazelle-like Russians! We were skunked by a superb team. During the game, however, the Vice President showed a distinct tendency to hog the shots, or to shout "let the colonel get it," while we were trying to protect the colonel's back from any shots. To our dismay Wallace roved all over the court with "I got it!" At the end, Wallace announced, "Now let's get a game with two Russian teams!" I discovered afterward that this so dismayed most of our American group that each did what I had done, simply, quietly, left the scene and returned to our quarters. The games continued for some time with hardly any Americans present.

★ ★ ★

The Russians were a source of considerable interest. There were about 200 officers and non-coms. The officers had access to our Ladd Field Officer's Club, but used it but little. A Russian Officer's Club had been provided for them in the former BOQ that had been assigned to them. The Base Theatre had a new bill about every 2-4 nights, and the shows included quite a number of the old "serials." Tom Mix, John Wayne, etc.. All the Russian-speaking Americans soon learned to wait to enter the theater after the lights had been dimmed. The reason: if Russians saw them enter, they immediately joined them, four or more in a bunch, and asked for running translations! Our men could not really see the show unless they slipped in after the theater was dark!

And the Russians could not understand the serials. At the end of one episode, our hero would be seen, unconscious in a mine car, for example, and the car would run right out of the tunnel into a mountainside to the rocks or river before. The next episode started with the scene the previous one had ended with, but from a different perspective, where our hero had awakened and jumped out just in time!

★ ★ ★

Russian officers wore beautiful, soft leather greatcoats, leather boots and belts, but would go into Fairbanks and buy up for shipment all the shoes they could get. I was in a shoe store on one occasion when a major came in with his aide. He asked for "shooss" and was asked "what kind," and he replied "all kinds." To "what size" he replied, "all sizes!" The merchant went to the rear of the store and brought hundreds of shoes and the colonel left his aide to complete the purchase. When I later asked the merchant about it, he told me that he had simply cleaned out all the "broken lines" that had accumulated over the years. He said he charged a fair price, but what the Russian paid he could never have got in ordinary shoe sales (a "broken" line is a line of various sizes that had been sold out of the more popular sizes, so that customers could not get their size, leaving the "odd sizes" literally unsaleable).

★ ★ ★

The pilots were great purchasers of perfume. The Ladd Field Officer's Mess, at lunch and dinner times, was "cafeteria style," with a "blue plate special." Waiting in line to go through the "chow line" were both U.S. and Russian officers. The Russians stood out with the perfume. I recall one rather small, blond-headed, wiry pilot. He smelled of Shalimar! We later learned from wiser heads that the perfume was not a "sissy" sign, but one of long-time uncleaned uniforms! This particular one certainly did not look to us like a combat pilot. It turned out that he had 26 Germans to his credit (Russian-style of counting) on the Western Front, from which his ALSIB ferry assignment was "R&R"!

★ ★ ★

They were, of course, allies. However, two incidents are of interest:

I received a call from the resident FBI agent, whose office was in the Post Office in Fairbanks, asking if I could meet with him in his office. His name, as I recall it, was Elmo Gaskin. When I met him he stated his familiarity with my assignment and duties and asked me what I could tell him about the Russians' capability to take information, equipment and material in and out of Alaska.

My reply was that the AACS handled their radio traffic, describing the two circuits over which we could communicate with Moscow; I told him that all their traffic (radio communications) were in their code and that we had no idea what was being said. Further,

they had aircraft coming and going from Russia—aircraft being ferried in the ALSIB program, and their own administrative aircraft (mostly C-47s) used to transport personnel and materiel in and out. He was incredulous, particularly when I stated that so far as I was aware, there were no restraints or restrictions on any of it. I said, "They are our allies!"

At the end of the war with Japan (V-J Day) I received a message, addressed to me, from the State Department in Washington asking me to ask the Russians for copies of what we would call "Facility Charts" covering airfields, were described as alternates for Tokyo, in connection with U.S. flights bringing in VIPs, etc., for the surrender ceremonies aboard the U.S.S. Missouri. I immediately communicated with my "opposite number," Captain Prokofsky, and was told that his was a very low echelon, that no such information was required in the performance of their duties, and that I should, instead, ask my State Department for the desired charts!

★ ★ ★

During my stay at Ladd Field, I was privilege to attend two Russian banquets, given in our Officer's Mess: the first was the observance of the second anniversary of the Russian presence at Ladd Field; the other was a Red Army Day celebration. After the anniversary party, to which I was the only one from our unit to be invited, and when several of us were invited to the Red Army Day party, I told my cohorts: "There will be flasks of vodka plus bottles of U.S. booze on each table. Restrain yourself and drink only when a Russian makes you drink!" Those at my table at the earlier event had helped themselves to our choice of the bottles of gin, bourbon and scotch that adorned each table (each sat 10). When the speechmaking and the frequent toasts began, we discovered that the little carafes (they appeared to be the kind usually used for oil and vinegar in restaurants) contained 150 proof vodka! We weathered the second party by following my admonition—but drank more than we were accustomed to anyway!

★ ★ ★

While on a visit with the Commanding Officer of the air base at Nome, I, our Nome Detachment Commander and Cryptographic Security Officer were invited to have drinks in the C.O.'s quarters. When we arrived, Colonel Vasin and several of his officers were there, along with several base officers. It was a most pleasant cocktail hour. As noted above, Colonel Vasin was very popular, spoke good English and displayed one of his many qualities as the time passed.

He designated one of his officers, a major, to serve the drinks and refills (with our C.O.'s agreement). As refills came along with what seemed like increasing regularity, we Americans began to feel we were about to disgrace our C.O.; we were beginning to wobble in our shoes. Colonel Vasin apparently observed our problem, spoke a few words in Russian to the major and no more drinks were served and our honor was preserved. It should be noted that one does not refuse to drink with a Russian; they really bear down if you seem to be declining a toast or another round!

CHAPTER SIX

SOLDIERS OF THE MIST—THE ALASKA TERRITORIAL GUARD

Major Marvin "Muktuk" Marston traveled by airplane, ... throughout the Arctic to organize the ... Scouts during World War Two. U.S. ARMY CENTER OF MILITARY HISTORY COLLECTION, WASHINGTON, D.C.

Territorial Governor Ernest Gruening organized the Alaska Territorial Guard after the Alaska National Guard was called to active duty in 1941. Gruening served longer than any other governor and became one of Alaska's two new senators when Alaska achieved statehood in 1959. ASL

Col. Jason P. Williams, a Spanish-American and World War One veteran, served as Adjutant General of the Alaska Territorial Guard during World War Two. ALASKA NATIONAL GUARD

Nearly every Eskimo village had an Alaska Scout unit of the ATG. They were Alaska's major defense effort along the coastline of the Bering Sea and the Arctic Ocean. UAA, OTTO GEIST COLL.

THIS SHELTER CABIN
is now being maintained by the
ALASKA TERRITORIAL GUARD
for the convenience of passers-by and for use in any
EMERGENCY

LEAVE WOOD AND KINDLING
for the next Traveler

KEEP CABIN CLEAN
BE CAREFUL OF FIRE

REPORT any repairs needed to
A. T. G. COMMANDER in next village.

The ATG maintained shelter cabins throughout rural Alaska. This sign gave directions to those who used the cabins. KRISTINE SCHUSTER

The ATG parades on Sitka's main street towards St. Michael's Cathedral during the war. There were ATG units in Southeastern Alaska, the Interior and in the territory's larger cities and towns as well as in the Arctic.
UAA, HANNA-CALL COLL.

The face of a scout. "Muktuk" Marston thinks of his World War Two Eskimo Scouts as he observes a new generation of Guardsmen at Camp Carroll in Anchorage. USA

Major Marston appoints a local citizen as company commander of an ATG Eskimo Scout unit. Many future Eskimo leaders were developed by the Territorial Guard. UAA, OTTO GEIST COLL.

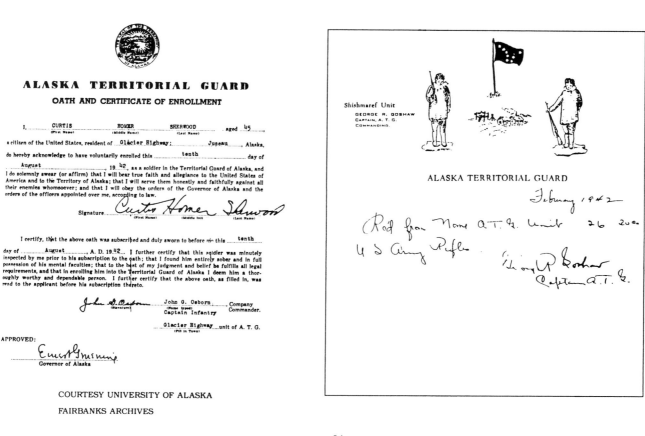

ALASKA TERRITORIAL GUARD

OATH AND CERTIFICATE OF ENROLLMENT

I, ___CURTIS___ ___HOMER___ ___SHERWOOD___ aged 45
   (First Name)   (Middle Name)   (Last Name)

a citizen of the United States, resident of ___Glacier Highway___; ___Juneau___, Alaska,

do hereby acknowledge to have voluntarily enrolled this ___tenth___ day of

___August___, 19 42, as a soldier in the Territorial Guard of Alaska, and I do solemnly swear (or affirm) that I will bear true faith and allegiance to the United States of America and to the Territory of Alaska; that I will serve them honestly and faithfully against all their enemies whomsoever; and that I will obey the orders of the Governor of Alaska and the orders of the officers appointed over me, according to law.

Signature ___Curtis Homer Sherwood___
    (First Name)   (Middle Init)   (Last Name)

I certify, that the above oath was subscribed and duly sworn to before me this ___tenth___ day of ___August___, A. D. 19 42. I further certify that this soldier was minutely inspected by me prior to his subscription to the oath; that I found him entirely sober and in full possession of his mental faculties; that to the best of my judgment and belief he fulfills all legal requirements, and that in enrolling him into the Territorial Guard of Alaska I deem him a thoroughly worthy and dependable person. I further certify that the above oath, as filled in, was read to the applicant before his subscription thereto.

___John G. Osborn___ ___John G. Osborn___, Company
    (Signature)   (Name typed)   Commander.
Captain Infantry

___Glacier Highway___unit of A. T. G.
    (Fill in Town)

APPROVED:

___Ernest Gruening___
Governor of Alaska

COURTESY UNIVERSITY OF ALASKA

FAIRBANKS ARCHIVES

Shishmaref Unit
GEORGE R. GOSHAW
CAPTAIN, A. T. G.
COMMANDING.

ALASKA TERRITORIAL GUARD

February 1942

Rec'd from Nome A.T.G. Unit 26 200
U.S. Army Rifles

George R. Goshaw
Captain A.T.G.

A unit of Marston's Tundra Army awaits inspection. The Eskimo Scouts were experts in spotting anything unusual in the Arctic and kept American forces informed.
ALASKA NATIONAL GUARD

Major Marston became a familiar figure in the Arctic during the war. He became a champion for Native People's rights following the war.
UAA, OTTO GEIST COLL.

"Muktuk" Marston enjoyed his years as commander of the ATG in the Arctic and formed a permanent bond with the Eskimo people.
UAA, OTTO GEIST COLL.

A unit of the Eskimo Scouts.
CLIFF SALISBURY

The U.S. Army sent artists to Alaska during the war to capture a human record of conflict. Joe Jones depicts Major Marston signing up Eskimos for the ATG.
U.S. ARMY ART COLL., WASHINGTON, D.C.

Henry Varnum Poor's painting "Eskimo Guerrillas" was done during his trip up the Arctic Coast with Major Marston. U.S. ARMY ART COLL., WASHINGTON, D.C.

CHAPTER SEVEN
ATTU

Japanese troops occupy Attu, June 1942.

The Battle For Attu

Rear Admiral F.W. Rockwell was appointed "Commander, Amphibious Force North Pacific," to conduct the landing at Attu. "Operation Landgrab," was the code name given to this invasion. Up to this time, the U.S. had undertaken only two other amphibious landings: Guadalcanal and North Africa. The 7th Infantry Division would make the landing, backed up by a strong naval force of three battleships, escort carrier, and numerous smaller ships.

The 11th Air Force operations plan was spelled out:

1. Ten days prior to D-Day (7 May) fighters were to intercept and destroy shipping. Take photographs of "Boodle" (Kiska) and "Jackboot" (Attu).

2. On D-5, they were to harass enemy garrisons and destroy installations on the islands.

On D-10, P-38's moved to Amchitka. The P-40's and P-38's would concentrate on Kiska. In ten days, 155 tons of bombs were dropped on Kiska and 96 tons on Attu. The 11th Air Force photographs were the only source of intelligence as to the Japanese strength and positions on the islands.

Weather plagued the invasion force. High winds created high seas, and tides making a landing, on time, almost impossible. The invasion was postponed till 9 May.

Weather on the 8th was still bad. The invasion was again postponed till May 11. The fog was so thick that navigation and ship separation were dependent on radar, which was new and not entirely reliable. One collision occurred, but both ships made it back to port.

On May 11, 1943, the 11th Air Force aircraft were dispersed as follows:

	P-40's	P-38's	B-25's	F-5's Navy	B-24's	Total
Umnak	35	1	1			37
Adak	22	1	10		12	45
Amchitka	23	24	20	3	15	86
Total	80	26	31	3	28	168

Two major landings were contemplated on Attu: one west of Holtz Bay, on the northern side of the island; the other in Massacre Bay, on the south side. By nightfall of the 11th, 1,500 troops were ashore on the north and 2,000 on the south. No enemy was encountered. The question was—where was the enemy?

The Missoula Sentinel

The Only Afternoon Paper in Western Montana With FULL ASSOCIATED PRESS News Service. Always Reliable.

STAMPS
Expires
May 30
May 31
May 31
May 31
May 31
June 15

U. S. WEATHER BUREAU FORECAST:
Little change in temperature today and tomorrow morning; showers this afternoon.
Thermometer:
Maximum ____54 Minimum ____32
At 9 a. m. ____36 Today noon ____43

III. NO. 60   MISSOULA, MONTANA, FRIDAY EVENING, MAY 14, 1943   PRICE FIVE CENTS

lian Bases Are Subjected to Terrific Pounding

YANKS MAKE BID FOR ATTU

German-Held Areas Hit Hard

Soldiers, Planes Are Battling Japs on Island

inia
Hit
oast Also in Bombers ng From Africa

ED KENNEDY
leadquarters in a, May 14.—(AP) r squadrons erful blows upon Sicily and Italy terday in an offenger divided by y for support of ps in Tunisia.

Fortresses and medelivered a smashing lgiari, port and air helped support Axis Africa. the biggest yet un-d Sardinian targets, that on Maddalena

ky vessels were sunk large oil fires were Sicilian harbor of out 50 U. S. Liber-s from Middle East aped almost 360,000 atives there under ort from Malta. Calabria and Mescities which felt the er unleashed by the surrender of the last veral Jurgin von men, a surrender ormous quantities of prisoners.
remain in North for prisoners in our communique said.

Senate Beats Down Two Amendments

Washington, May 14.—(AP) With bi-partisan advocates of the "skip-a-year" plan of tax abatement holding their lines firmly, the Senate beat down, 57 to 21, today an administration attempt to amend the tax revenue bill to provide for cancellation of only 75 per cent of a year's levies.

The vote, on an amendment offered by Chairman George, Democrat, Georgia, of the Senate Finance committee, cleared the way for an expected early vote on a modified version of the Ruml plan under which the taxes would be excused for all persons to put them on a current payment basis.

Earlier the Senate rejected, 57 to 31, an amendment to credit current payments against the year's income and collect the full 1942 tax in 16 semi-annual installments beginning next March 15.

Trailers, Trucks To Be Built
For Alcan Road

Berlin One Victim Of Raids

Ruhr, Czecho-Slovakia, France Hit in 48-Hour Aerial Assault

BY THE ASSOCIATED PRESS

London, May 14.—Berlin, Czechoslovakia and the Ruhr valley of Germany were pounded in great strength by British bombers last night and the Berlin radio reported that four-engined American bombers had attacked the North German coastal area at noon today, extending the augmented Allied air offensive to nearly 48 hours of incessant assault.

Soldiers, Planes Are Battling Japs on Island

BY JOHN M. HIGHTOWER

Washington, May 14.—(AP)—The United States has launched the long-expected attack to drive Japan out of the Aleutian islands.

American troops landed on the island of Attu Tuesday, the Navy announced today, and were met by Japanese of unknown strength.

They are locked in battle now.

The situation still is not clear, but United States air and sea forces presumably are participating in an all-out bid for early decision.

Attu so far appears to be the only direct target of American landings. A general conclusion that no similar attack has been made yet on Kiska, the other Japanese Aleutian base, was based in part on the fact that a communique today told of fresh air attacks on that island.

The landing was announced in Navy communique No. 376, which said:

"North Pacific:

"1. On May 11 United States forces landed at the island of Attu in the Aleutians, and are now engaged with Japanese forces on the island. Details of the operation will be released when the situation clarifies."

Naval spokesmen declined to go beyond the limits of this bare announcement or offer any comment on the course of the fighting.

Hitler Expected

Aleutian islands, showing Attu, scene of battle as U. S. forces land in effort to drive out the Japanese

Landing 5-11-1943

The Japanese commander, Colonel Yamazaki, had only 2,634 men on Attu. He had twelve anti-aircraft guns and a few coastal guns. He decided not to split his force but to concentrate it in blockading the valley connecting Massacre and Holtz Bays. Colonel Yamazaki prepared to sell Attu dearly.

P-38's provided air cover on D-Day. They also strafed and dropped bombs in support of the ground troops.

The action in the Aleutians forced the Japanese to draw some of their capital ships from the Southern Fleet to support the Northern Fleet. This gave Admiral Turner an unopposed landing at Rendova, in the Solomon Islands, in June.

The U.S. war ships supported the landing on Attu by shelling the island and patrolling for possible Japanese ships.

The soldiers ashore found the going tough. The muskeg and underlying mud made walking difficult, and it was almost impossible for trucks and tractors to move.

The Japanese launched nineteen torpedo carrying planes from Paramushiro on 22 May, and surprised the United States ships *Phelps* and *Charleston*. The two ships put up a terrific chatter of anti-aircraft fire and maneuvered so violently, that they evaded all the torpedoes. They shot down one plane and damaged another. The returning Japanese planes reported sinking both ships.

The next day, 23 May, the Japanese tried another air raid. Sixteen planes, from Paramushiro, were intercepted by P-38's from Amchitka. In the ensuing battle, four enemy planes were shot down and eight damaged. The Japanese planes were forced to jettison their bombs harmlessly in the ocean.

Between 19 and 25 May, the Japanese, under Colonel Yamazaki, retreated onto a fishhook shaped ridge by Chichagof Harbor. The 11th Air Force dropped surrender leaflets but none of the Japanese surrendered. On 29 May, the Japanese staged a massive "Banzai" charge. A thousand strong, the Japanese attacked, yelling "Japanese drink blood like wine." The Japanese over-ran command posts and medical stations. They were finally stopped by a detachment of Army engineers. This attack was the end of organized resistance on Attu.

Results of the ground battle were: over 2,300 Japanese killed, and 29 prisoners; over 500 U.S. soldiers killed, and 1,200 wounded.

As soon as the serious fighting on Attu was over, the engineers landed and built an airstrip on the east side of the island. The engineers, also, went ashore on the island of Shemya, twenty-five miles east of Attu. Shemya is four miles long and the only flat island in the Aleutians. The engineers started to construct an airfield 10,000 feet long, for B-29's which were programmed to arrive in about six months. The B-29's were going to be used to bomb the Kurile Islands. (B-29's were not used in this operation.)

One method the Japanese used to replace their aircraft losses at Kiska was to ship them to Attu where they were flown the rest of the way to Kiska. The aerial photo, taken Nov. 7, 1942, at Holtz Bay, shows four Rufes in a cove at Attu. AAF

Kawanishi E7K2 Navy Type 94, Allied code name Alf, at Chichagof Harbor. It was probably this reconnaissance float plane that flew over the Aleut village during the early morning landing of the Japanese.
JAPANESE PHOTO VIA
LARRY GOLDEN

KHS THELMA MADSEN COLL.

The oblique, aerial photograph of Chichagof Habor was taken on Sept. 21, 1942, according to the legend at the bottom. The numbers are the work of a photo interpreter to point out various items of interest. One, two and nine are Attu Village. USA

Coxswains of landing boats receive instructions from Capt. Herbert B. Knowles, USN, shipper of the USS *Heywood* (APA6) en route to Attu, May 4, 1943. The large relief map was elevated to shoulder height to obtain a more natural view of the beach as it would appear to the boats when the landings were made. NA 80-G-50689

LANDING

CHICHAGOF
HARBOR

EMPTY AA GUN
EMPLACEMENTS

GROUND
EXCAVATIONS FOR
BUILDINGS

ATTU VILLAGE

CHURCH

LANDING BARGES

EMPTY GUN
EMPLACEMENTS

TRENCH
SYSTEMS

This mosaic, made up from vertical aerial photographs taken at an altitude of 5,000 feet, shows Attu Village, a bomb burst near it, empty Japanese buildings and gun revetments. USA

Mosaic of Holtz Bay showing Japanese landing barges, destroyed float planes and tents. 11TH AIR FORCE

Aboard the USS *Bell* on May 12, 1943. The cameraman riding in the rear of a landing barge was able to get a fine shot of part of the first group of barges as they proceeded to shore. In some places the fog was so heavy that it was impossible for the photographer to see more than one barge.

Landing barges circling in fog before approaching the shore in the first assault wave.

This photograph of the Chichagof Harbor, far left, and Holtz Bay, center, was taken from Colonel Eareckson's B-24 on May 12.
LARRY REINEKE COLL.

Troops leave the attack transport *Heywood* (APA-6) the afternoon of May 11 for the beaches of Attu. USA

Replacement troops move up from the beach into battle. USA

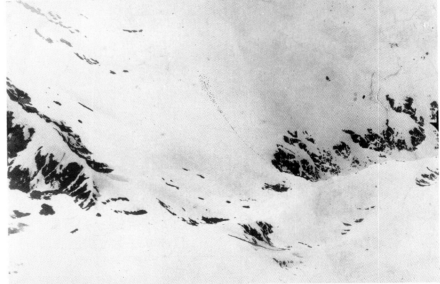

The Japanese can be seen as small dots as they make their way up a snow field toward Chichagof Harbor following the order to evacuate the Holtz Bay area.
BERTRAND HOAK COLL.

Attu was an infantryman's war that tested the spirits and souls of all those engaged in the battle. USA

Mortar crew. 11TH AIR FORCE

Mortar crew, Massacre Bay. ASL US ARMY SIGNAL CORPS PCA 175-58

A carrier-based Navy F4F coming out of the fog in a spin,
about to crash on Attu, May 14, 1943. 11TH AIR FORCE

Observation post overlooking Massacre Bay.
ASL US ARMY SIGNAL CORPS PCA 175-57

Artillery fire at Massacre Bay. ASL, US ARMY SIGNAL CORPS PCA 175-60

Some of the few Japanese prisoners taken at Attu.
KANSAS STATE HISTORICAL SOCIETY, US ARMY SIGNAL CORPS

Japanese Dead and Captured

When American forces moved into the Holtz Bay area, over 100 Japanese soldiers were found dead in their barracks and around the area. This soldier was wounded but fought to the end.

In the last days of the battle several Japanese prisoners were taken. Instead of being killed—as the Japanese believed they would be—they were treated very well, fed and treated medically. Later they were taken to the command post and questioned. A few of the Japanese spoke some English.

The more serious casualties from the battle were removed from the field hospital to the USS *St. Mihiel* for further medical attention. They were later taken to Adak. A cradle was lowered into the landing barge and the patient and stretcher were placed in it and hoisted aboard ship.

Chaplain Ruben Curtis leads men in singing hymns at a burial service for soldiers killed at Massacre Bay, June 1, 1943. Each grave held six bodies. ASL, U.S. ARMY SIGNAL CORPS COLL.

The bodies of Americans were collected and taken to a cemetery in the rear where they were made ready for burial.

Japanese Remains

Japanese barracks.

Japanese heavy machine gun.

Japanese tractor. KANSAS STATE HISTORICAL SOCIETY

Japanese steam roller used for airfield construction. KANSAS STATE HISTORICAL SOCIETY

A Rufe, float–type Zero fighter, riddled by shells, is dragged onto the Holtz Bay beach.

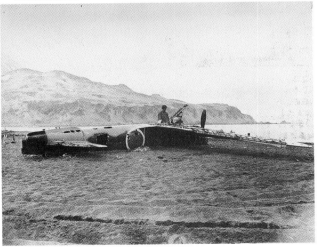

A Rufe which had crashed earlier in the year on the beach.

A Japanese landing craft.

When the Americans entered Chichagof Harbor they occupied a tent camouflaged with rocks and thick walls of tundra and dirt, which had been used by the Japanese as their headquarters. With the capture of the Chichagof area the last of the main Japanese forces were defeated and the battle was over.

Shortly before Chichagof Bay was taken, the Japanese in the area, realizing they were trapped, pulled out with all their able men. Those who were disabled and unable to leave were killed by the Japanese themselves or allowed to commit suicide. The Japanese attacked the American lines and broke through the portion of the line located on the high ground overlooking the corridor between Chichagof and Sarana bays. This is an American kitchen raided by the attacking enemy troops.

On the northwest end of the beach several Japanese barracks and supply depots, camouflaged against the side of the hill, were found. These were constructed of wood and covered with tundra and rocks. From a short distance they were almost invisible to the eye.

Japanese gun left on the island.

Massive amounts of supplies were put ashore the day after the initial landings. KANSAS STATE HISTORICAL SOCIETY

When the Americans moved into the Holtz Bay area they cleaned out a captured Japanese barracks and converted it into a telephone center.

Burial site for 34 enemy soldiers on Attu. All the Japanese were eventually exhumed and returned to Japan. 11TH AIR FORCE

The American Red Cross was active on Attu after the island was secure. Here Mr. H.D. Roberts, Red Cross field director, walks with Coxswain Enok Hansen of Ketchikan in August 1943. AMERICAN RED CROSS

Company "A"
383rd Port Battalion (TC)

This military unit, the only Black outfit that participated in the Attu campaign, has been a neglected story. According to Benjamin M. Woods, an NCO in the unit, it was transported to the Aleutians in April 1943 on the Army transport *Grant*. It was deployed by landing craft into Massacre Bay and onto Yellow Beach on May 13 early into the battle for Attu. The unit was one of the supporting units assigned to the 7th Infantry Division and many of the approximately 200 troops had previous training in stevedore duties, infantry tactics, field artillery and engineers. Mr. Woods has worked for years to get his outfit recognized as the **only** Black unit involved in the Attu campaign.

"Beanies" knitted at home by members of the Volunteer Production Corps of the American Red Cross are distributed by Field Director H.D. Roberts to members of the 383rd Port Battalion, based on Attu. AMERICAN RED CROSS

Little Falls Cemetery, September 1943. 11TH AIR FORCE

Radio Intercept Station at Murder Point, 1943.

Attu 1945

Photos from Dale Luttmann of the 77th Bomb Squadron

B-25s over and on
Attu, 1945. DALE LUTTMANN

B-25s of the 77th Bomb
Squadron. DALE LUTTERMANN

V-J day on Attu. DALE LUTTMANN

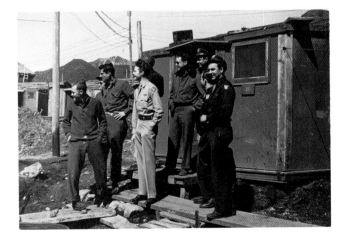

ALASKA FLYERS RAID JAP CONVOY IN KURILE ISLES

11TH AIR FORCE HDQ., Aleutians,, May 11 [Delayed] — (AP) — American army flyers sank at least one Japanese ship, damaged two more, including a warship, and barely missed a 7,000 ton troop transport today during a raid on Kataoka navy base, Shumushu, in the Kurile Islands of northern Japan.

Officers said it was possible an air-sea battle was still raging in that area.

Enemy vessels sunk or damaged included a 2,500 ton cargo ship blown up and destroyed, and a frigate and a freighter. One Mitchell bomber, hit by flak, blew up in the air.

South of Kataoka, navy search planes in two flights strafed and fired rockets into Japanese radar installations at Minami cape on eastern Paramushiro.

Surprise Jap Convoy

Mitchell bombers and Liberators surprised an enemy convoy, which sneaked into Kataoka presumably under cover of fog. The Liberators dropped a score of 150 pound general purpose bombs from medium altitude.

The fog lifted as the American planes arrived over the target to find the convoy of 13 ships, including warship escorts, stretched over a two mile area from Kataoka harbor to Kashiwabara, troop staging area on northern Paramushiro.

Five Japanese fighters made half-hearted attacks on one flight of Mitchells, but the Americans drove them off.

Kuriles Reёnforced

The convoy was the largest spotted in these waters since Sept. 11, 1943, when Aleutians based flyers surprised Japanese Kurile bases for the first time in the war.

Presence of troop transports, plus cargo vessels in the convoy indicated that Japan may have decided to reёnforce the northern Kuriles, which lie south of the tip of Siberian Kamchatka. This was also the first large scale sea movement noted in this area since Russia denounced its neutrality treaty with Japan.

Shemya, just east of Attu, was a major bomber base for the Kurile Islands operations in 1944 and '45. HARRY ELEGREET

Crew photo in front of B-24L #44-49863, which they brought up to Shemya from Hamilton Field, California. In September 1945 a crew using it to pick up "flying time" crashed it on Alaid Island, killing all on board. HARRY ELEGREET

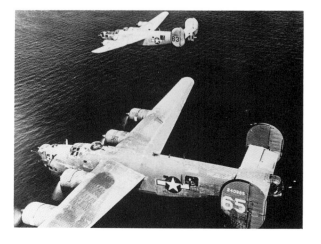

B-24s of the 404th Bombardment Squadron over the Aleutians. HARRY ELEGREET

Japanese weapons captured on Attu.
KANSAS STATE HISTORICAL SOCIETY

These are the new T.99 rifles
of 7.7mm (31) that replaced
the T.38 6.5mm (25) models
and were seen on Attu for
the first time.

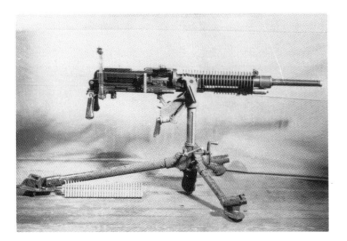

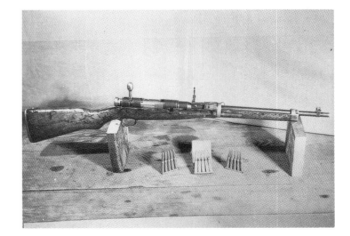

Japanese weapons captured on Attu. On the left is a T.92 machine gun and on the right a T.38 Engineer's carbine.
THOMAS LANGAN

Attu Today

The rusting hulks on the beach at Murder Point are grim reminders of what happened here. Note one of the docks in the distance and, beyond that, Alexai Point where the American airfield was located on the Massacre Bay side of the Island.

At Holtz Bay, the site of the Japanese encampment, all that is visible above the canopy of tundra is a rusting bulldozer. The foundation of many of the buildings can only be found the hard way, by falling into them, as the tundra is so green and leafy that a walker cannot see the ground.

Attu has the most easterly junkyard in the United States. When the military left the island, it simply bulldozed all of the buildings and equipment into the sea. Just off Murder Point there is a good mile of debris, which includes treads, vehicles, landing craft, bottles, chains, tires, cooking utensils and every other artifact of the American occupation of the island.

The most plentiful reminders of the importance of Attu are the rusting piles of "Marston Matting." Just before World War II, experiments were conducted on an innovative landing mat that would allow airstrips to appear, quite literally, overnight in jungles as well as on sand and muskeg. The result was Marston Matting, named for the city in North Carolina in which the product was manufactured.

ALL PHOTOS COURTESY OF STEVE LEVI OF ANCHORAGE, ALASKA

Several deteriorating docks are evidence that Attu was once a heavily populated air base. Today the docks are no longer connected to the shoreline. In the background is one of the ships that occasionally does scientific research in the waters surrounding Attu.

On the road to Engineer's Ridge, holes where ammunition depots used to stand can be seen in one of the arms of Peaceful Valley.

Most of the quonsets have collapsed under the weight of snow. In many places, the mist makes the abandoned city appear eerie.

Oddly, wood structures outlast the quonsets. This one, at the entrance to Peaceful Valley, still had its wiring intact as well as a few windows.

A U.S. 100-lb. practice bomb on Attu.

The most dangerous ordnance on Attu are the burster shells. This one, probably live, was in the ammunition dump, off limits to personnel without proper clearance.

In front of the LORSTA Attu is a plaque in memory of those Americans who gave their lives on Attu.

The last of the landing craft that offloaded Americans at Massacre Bay.

On the crest of Engineer Hill are three monuments and a plaque. Two of the monuments are in Japanese, and the third is a massive steel structure that has flags which can be cranked out on ceremonial occasions.

Beached on a lonely bend of the Temnac River five miles inland are the remains of a P-38 fighter.

There is no doubt that the pilot of the P-38 walked away from the crash.

A Japanese roller used on the airfield in the Holtz Bay area. KHS

American equipment left on Attu after the war. BLAINE CORNELISON

A massive amount of wire is still in evidence on the island.

A possible Japanese anti-aircraft gun mount.

Japanese guns and a propeller overlooking the harbor.

The Attu International Airport.

A U.S. Coast Guard Loran Station is the only military presence on Attu today.

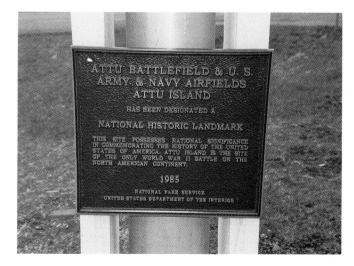

A Coast Guard C-130 from Kodiak supplies Attu every few weeks. Charter flights for bird fanciers are flown to the island every year by Reeve Aleutian Airways.

Attu Memorial Honors Those Killed in WWII

ENGINEER HILL, ATTU ISLAND—Dignitaries from Japan and the United States joined here last week to honor those killed in action during a World War II battle, second only to Iwo Jima in terms of troops involved during South Pacific fighting.

The 18-foot Attu Island Peace Memorial was placed on the ridge of Engineer Hill, the site of the last desperate battle for control of the only North American land involved in World War II. The hill is still pock-marked by foxholes and pillboxes dug during the fighting on the island.

The titanium memorial topped by miniature replicas of flags from Alaska, Japan and the United States, was designed and placed on Attu by Sumitomo Metal Industries Ltd. of Japan.

The ceremony was highlighted by dedications of wreaths from the Prime Minister of Japan and the White House. It ran deep with emotion when the son of U.S. Infantry platoon Sgt. Alejandro Montanez Sr., who was killed during the battle, met with the son of a Japanese Medical Corps commander who was killed on the battle site.

The two men, Alejandro Montanez Jr., commander of the U.S. Public Health Service, and Tomoyuki Omura, manager of Sumitomo Ltd., shared pictures of their parents and talked of feelings about the memorial.

"We can't communicate with languages," said Montanez, "But I think he got the feeling it was more than a handshake."

"Let's hope we never have to do this again," Montanez said to Omura as they placed photographs of their parents underneath a plaque dedicated by the Japanese to Omura's father and the medical corps which served on the island.

Yasuyuki Yamazaki, son of Col. Yasugo Yamazaki—the Japanese leader who was killed on Engineer Hill in the last skirmish of the battle—was also present at the ceremony. Yamazaki placed a wreath before the memorial.

Attu, after the war, was declared a Maritime National Wildlife Refuge, and 1,800 acres of it belong to the Coast Guard.

Among the Japanese dignitaries who spoke during the dedication, was Eijiro Hata, parliamentary vice minister for Japan's Ministry of Health and Welfare.

"As I stand here now and recall those days, I cannot feel but bitter mortification," Hata said.

Hata then pledged allegiance between Japan and other nations. "I solemnly swear that our nation will continue to maintain pacifism as its national guideline," he said.

Brig. Gen. Edward Belyea, chief of staff, Alaska Air National Guard, was present to dedicate a chrysanthemum and salute the peace monument.

"We are here to pay tribute to the lasting peace which exists between Japan and the U.S.," he said in his speech at the ceremony.

The inscription reads: "In memory of all those who sacrificed their lives in the islands and seas of the North Pacific during World War II and in dedication to world peace." The peace memorial was constructed by cooperation of the governments of both Japan and the United States, and it replaces a wooden one placed on the island by the Japanese in 1978.

—*Tundra Times*, July 6, 1987

An Alaska National Guard C-130 sits on the runway at Attu with a Japanese relic of World War II in the foreground. The C-130 brought the dignitaries to Attu for dedication of the Japanese Peace Memorial.

The Japanese Peace Memorial dedicated in July 1987 on Engineer Hill.

北太平洋戦没者の碑

さきの大戦において
太平洋の諸島及び海域で
戦没した人々をしのび
平和への思いをこめてこの碑を建立する

竣工 昭和62年7月1日 日本国政府 協力 アメリカ合衆国政府

IN MEMORY OF ALL THOSE WHO SACRIFICED
THEIR LIVES IN THE ISLANDS AND
SEAS OF THE NORTH PACIFIC
DURING WORLD WAR II AND
IN DEDICATION TO WORLD PEACE
CONSTRUCTED BY THE GOVERNMENT OF JAPAN
IN COOPERATION WITH
THE GOVERNMENT OF THE UNITED STATES OF AMERICA
ON 1 JULY 1987

Alejandro Montanez, center, and Tomoyuki Omura, right, share photographs and talk about memories of their fathers.

A former Japanese cave, shells and a written memorial to a Japanese soldier participant.

LCIs unload infantry on the rocky shore of Kiska.

NA 111-SC-341663

Three of the seaplanes from the 1934 U.S. Navy expedition on the beach at Kiska Harbor. Note the fox trapper cabins. The last trapper, a man and his daughter, left Kiska Island in April 1942. A Navy Seabee unit built two ranch-style houses and a generator shed 300-yards from the shore line in 1941. It housed a Navy weather detachment. The Japanese established the seaplane ramp on this beach and built their main camp behind it. USN

Japanese Occupation of Kiska

As part of a general offensive against United States bases in the Central and North Pacific, the Japanese in June 1942 invaded Alaskan waters with a large amphibious task force. In addition to cruisers, destroyers, and submarines of the Fifth Fleet, the enemy force included heavy and light cruisers and two aircraft carriers.

On 2 June the two enemy carriers were reported less than 400 miles south of Kiska. Although the weather front, under cover of which the enemy moved eastward, prevented anything but the most fragmentary and hazardous air reconnaissance, all available planes of the 11th Air Force were immediately ordered forward to what were then Alaska's secret and westernmost airfields, at Cold Bay and Fort Glenn.

On 3 June, and again on 4 June, carrier-based enemy bombers and fighters attacked Dutch Harbor. Unfavorable weather defeated all efforts to destroy either the enemy carriers or their convoying warships. But the interception of Japanese carrier-based fighters by United States planes at Cold Bay and Fort Glenn indicated to the enemy for the first time the existence of airfields west of Kodiak, a factor for which the Japanese were not prepared. This tactical surprise, plus continuing Japanese reverses at Midway which was then being attacked, induced the enemy to withdraw.

Meanwhile, to the west, the No. 3 Maizuru Special Landing Party, composed of 500 marines commanded by Lieutenant Commander Mukai Hifumi, occupied Kiska Island on 6 June 1942. Having captured all but one of the small ten-man naval detachment operating the United States Weather Station on Kiska, the Japanese set up headquarters in the weather station buildings and started construction of antiaircraft positions on North Head and in the Main Camp Area. At the same time some twenty vessels moved into Kiska Harbor, including the cruisers "Kiso" and "Tama" of the Fifth Fleet, three destroyers, three corvettes, three minesweepers, three hydrographic vessels, and four transports—the "Awata Maru," the "Kamagawa Maru," the "Asaka Maru," and the "Nissan Maru."

Failure to receive the usual reports from the Naval Weather Station on Kiska after 7 June indicated probable enemy action in that area, but it was not until 11 June that weather permitted air reconnaissance of the Western Aleutians. On that date enemy occupation of Kiska was confirmed.

On 12 June, 11th Air Force heavy bombers made their first bombing runs over the island, hitting and setting fire to two cruisers and one destroyer. Heavy anti-aircraft fire, which on this day as for some time to come, was heavier from warships in the harbor than from land batteries, brought down one Liberator. Twelve enemy seaplanes, four of them heavy four-motored "Kawanishi" flying boats, were also spotted within the harbor near Trout Lagoon. On the same day, aerial reconnaissance confirmed enemy occupation of Attu Island, and Radio Tokyo announced the acquisition of two Japanese bases in the Western Aleutians.

On 18 June, the "Nissan Maru" was hit and left sinking in Kiska Harbor. The first photographic sortie, flown 21 June confirmed this sinking. That the enemy was active during this period is indicated by the fact that between 21 June when the first photos were obtained and 26 June when a second photo sortie was flown, enemy installations on Kiska doubled in number. On 4 July, two United States submarines reported the sinking of three and possibly four enemy destroyers, three of them in Reynard Cove, Kiska, one off Cape Sabak, Agattu. On 7 August, United States warships shelled Kiska Harbor and on 30 August the first Japanese Prisoners of War taken in the Alaskan theater were captured. These were five surviving crew members of an enemy submarine destroyed on that date.

The three paragraphs above suggest the pattern of events for the remainder of the summer of 1942 — sporadic bombing and strafing missions over Kiska and Attu whenever weather permitted, and occasional submarine attacks on Japanese shipping in Aleutian waters. The enemy, in turn, bombed Nazan Bay, Atka, on 14 June, and reconnoitered Adak on both 20 and 23 June. The race for possession of Adak and other intervening islands suitable for land-based aviation commenced.

During August the enemy reinforced its Kiska garrison with a second naval landing party of approximately 1,000 marines and with a civilian construction crew of approximately 500 laborers. These new units, together with the resident No. 3 Maizuru Special Landing Party, were organized into the No. 5 Defense Force under command of Navy Captain Sato. This No. 5 Defense Force occupied and manned an inner ring of defensive positions around Kiska Harbor, extending from Little Kiska through South Head, the Submarine Base, and the Main Camp to North Head. At about this same time, Kiska was re-designated the "51st Naval Base" and placed under the command of Rear Admiral Akiyama, who reached the island some time in the late summer or early fall of 1942.

On 31 August, United States Forces landed on Adak, and by 12 September had completed construction of an airfield there. The tempo of air attacks on Kiska was immediately accelerated. The first raid of major proportions conducted from Adak was 14 September, when

hits were reported on three large cargo vessels, two mine-sweepers were sunk, and three midget submarines and one four-motored "Kawanishi" flying boat were strafed. The enemy retaliated with token raids over Adak on 3 and 4 October.

In mid-September, the 301st Independent Infantry Battalion commanded by Major Hozumi Matsutoshi, formerly the 1st Battalion of the 26th Infantry Regiment, 7th Division, Hokkaido, moved from Attu, which it had occupied since June, to Gertrude Cove, Kiska. United States air reconnaissance first reported the withdrawal from Attu on 22 September and the occupation of Gertrude Cove on 1 October. By this latter date, there were huts, tents, gun installations and a small road net in Gertrude Cove. On 16 October, planes over Gertrude Cove sank a freighter; and on the same date, six "Marauders" sank one enemy destroyer and damaged another off Sirius Point, Kiska.

Japanese fighter and reconnaissance plane replenishments arrived boxed and crated on the decks of small plane transports. One such ship, working the Aleutian run, was the "Kimikawa Maru," which carried seven to nine planes per trip. The planes were sometimes unloaded and assembled at Attu, to be flown to Kiska when circumstances and weather were favorable; on other occasions, they were brought direct to Kiska and assembled there. By air combat and strafing of moored planes, the 11th Air Force whittled the enemy's air strength down about as fast as he could bring new planes in. For example, on 29 September, 5 enemy fighters were shot down over Kiska, and on 5 October, 6 more were shot down. At no time during the enemy's hold on Kiska did his total effective plane strength exceed fourteen planes, and usually it was so much lower than this figure that he avoided combat.

In late November, and while it was still west of Attu, United States Naval search planes picked up an enemy convoy carrying a force for the occupation of the Semichis. Frightened by possible air attack the convoy returned to Paramushiro and the component units of the force were re-assigned to Attu and Kiska. As a result, the 302nd Independent Infantry Battalion plus the 32nd Independent Antiaircraft Company, a company or more of the 26th Shipping Engineer Regiment, and units of the Nagamine Anchorage Headquarters all reached Kiska in December or January to reinforce Army and Navy units already there. The Shipping Engineer and Anchorage units went to Kiska Harbor, the 302nd to the Gertrude Cove area.

A reconnaissance party returning from Amchitka in December 1942 reported evidence of recent Japanese patrols on Amchitka. The enemy patrols had dug test holes on several sites suitable for airfields..

Two 5,000-ton enemy cargo vessels were sunk

through combined efforts of the 11th Air Force and Navy on 5 January.

On 12 January 1943, United States forces occupied Amchitka. It was almost two weeks, or 24 January, before the enemy planes attacked. During the next few days, whenever weather permitted, the enemy scouted and bombed Amchitka. The bombing was light and inaccurate, however, and ceased when "Warhawks" and "Lightnings" landed on the new Amchitka fighter strip on 17 February. The occupation of Amchitka, like the occupation of Adak five months before, permitted an immediate acceleration of bombing and reconnaissance missions over Kiska and Attu, and within two months had forced the enemy to abandon his efforts to bring supplies by surface vessels into Kiska and Attu. The 3rd of March saw the first single-engine bombing raid on Kiska with "Warhawks" and "Lightnings" loaded with anything up to one 1,000-lb. demolition bomb each. from Amchitka. From that date on, it was SOP to bomb Kiska with "Warhawks" and "Lightnings" loaded with anything up one 1,000-lb demolition bomb each.

Photos of 19 January revealed the beginnings of an enemy fighter strip south of Salmon Lagoon, Kiska. This strip, and another strip begun about the same time on Attu, were the target of constant attack throughout the spring. Partially as a result of these attacks, and partially because they lacked adequate machinery, the Japanese failed to finish either airfield although the construction schedule called for completion of the Kiska runway in March and for completion of the Attu runway shortly thereafter.

During the naval shelling of Attu on 18 February, an enemy ammunition ship was destroyed.

The organization of the North Sea Defense Headquarters with two Sectors—Sector One at Kiska and Sector Two at Attu—may or may not have coincided with the arrival of Major General Mineki Toichiro, at Kiska in the early spring of 1943. At the time of his arrival, tactical command of the Kiska and Attu garrisons was transferred from the Imperial Navy's Fifth Fleet to the hands of Lieutenant General Higuchi, Kiichiro, commanding officer of the Northern Army

The Navy weather and radio station at Kiska Harbor where William House and his companions kept their lonely vigil. The PBYs in the harbor were probably flown by Russell and Coleman during their visit to the station in late May. North Head where the Japanese established a major defensive system is clearly visible. The two ranch-style houses and the generator shed between them that provided power and heat were built by a Seabee unit. The other buildings belonged to fox trappers. A number of buildings were maintained around the island for supporting the harvesting of the foxes that had been artificially introduced to Kiska and other Aleutian Islands as one of the means of providing an economy for the island inhabitants. The last trappers, a man and his daughter, left the island around April 1942. USN

The Kiska Weather Detachment. Front row, from left to right: Ships Cook Third Class J.C. McCandless, Radioman Third Class R. Christensen, Aerographers Mate Third Class W.M. Winfrey, Seaman Second Class G.T. Palmer, Aerographers Mate Second Class W.I. Gaffney. Second row, from left to right: Aerographers Mate Second Class J.L. Turner, Chief Pharmacy Mate R.L. Copperfield, Aerographers Mate First Class William C. House, Lieutenant Mull, Radioman Second Class L.L. Eccles, Chief Pharmacy Mate L. Yaconelli and Radioman Third Class M.L. Courtney. Lieutenant Mull and Chief Yaconelli were from the *Casco*. The dog, Explosion, had been given to the men earlier by Ensign William C. Jones, a radio technician who helped set up the radio. The dog got her name from the fact that she had been born the night that a small, dynamite storage shack at Dutch Harbor had exploded nearby. When the Americans and Canadians reoccupied the island a year later, she was there to greet them. The photograph was taken just prior to the departure of the *Casco*. HOWARD R. CURTIS COLL.

Left to right: RM 3/C Christiansen and AERM 3/C Winfrey operating radio equipment at the Kiska Weather Station, Dec. 26, 1941. USN NH 70058

Two of the weather station personnel taken prisoner on Kiska. USMC #315172

Surf conditions in Kiska Harbor wreaked havoc with the Japanese float planes. These are two Nakajima A6M2-N float fighters. LARRY GOLDEN

Japanese light cruisers of the *Nagara* and *Kuma* class in Kiska Harbor, June 1942. 11TH AIR FORCE

The *INS Ikazuchi* DD57 or *INS Inazuma* DD58, part of the 6th Destroyer Division.

The Aichi E13A1 Jake twin float reconnaissance plane was one of several types of aircraft the Japanese used on Kiska. It also was used for search and rescue, as a transport aircraft and in a limited attack role. Its 1,298 range proved useful in the Aleutians. It was armed with one light machine gun and could carry 551 pounds of bombs. The Jake accommodated a crew of three. The photographs show how the Japanese shipped their aircraft to Kiska. JAPANESE PHOTOS VIA LARRY GOLDEN

Japanese float plane pilots being briefed on the beach at Kiska. A Jake can be seen in the background.

U.S. Bombing of Japanese At Kiska Island Resumed

Washington, Feb. 10.—(P)—Bombing attacks on Japanese at Kiska in the Aleutian islands in the North Pacific were reported by the Navy today in a communique which told also of aerial activity in the Solomons, possibly preceding the withdrawal of Japanese from Guadalcanal.

Results of the aerial activity in the Aleutians were not reported.

The communique number 276:

"North Pacific:

"1. On February 8 Liberator heavy bombers (Consolidated B-24) and Mitchell medium bombers (North American B-25) dropped bombs on the enemy camp area at Kiska and on installations at North Head. Seven flat-type Zeros were observed on the water but no attempt to intercept was made. All United States planes returned.

"South Pacific (All dates are East longitude):

"2. On February 9:

"(a) Airacobra fighters (Bell P-39) strafed and sank an enemy barge off Hooper bay in the Northern Russell islands. A number of floating drums of fuel oil were destroyed in the same vicinity.

"(b) During the evening a force of Maurauder medium bombers (Martin B-26) with Airacobra and Lightning (Lockheed P-38) escort bombed Japanese positions on Kolombangara island in the New Georgia group. Results were not reported.

"(c) During the evening Dauntless dive bombers (Douglas) with Lightning and Wildcat (Grumman F4F) escort attacked Japanese positions at Munda on New Georgia island. A large fire was started.

"(e) United States ground forces on Guadalcana island advanced to positions one-half mile west of the Segilau river in the vicinity of Doma Cova. On the northwest coast of the island United States troops advanced to the northeast as far as Visale. No opposition was encountered. A large amount of enemy equipment was captured."

with headquarters at Sapporo in Hokkaido.

March and April 1943, saw increasingly severe bombing attacks on Kiska and Attu, with the latter getting more attention as D-day for the assault on Attu approached. On 24 April, between Attu and Russia's Komandorski Islands, a light United States naval force engaged a heavier enemy fleet and foiled an effort to run two supply vessels into Attu or Kiska. This was the last known effort to supply either enemy garrison by surface vessels.

Bad weather and the preoccupation of all arms with operations on Attu gave the Kiska garrison a respite during May. But with the reduction of Attu completed in early June, the attack on Kiska was resumed. During June and July the vigor of this attack mounted almost daily. Simultaneously, the evidence of enemy submarine activity in waters around Kiska increased. On 11 June, one enemy submarine was sunk; on 13 June., another; and on 22 June, a third.

On 8 June, Rear Admiral Akiyama issued an order to the Kiska garrison instructing units to be ready for evacuation to an unnamed point "X." Beginning with photographs taken from 22 July on, evidence of what might be preparations for evacuation were noted. This evidence included the destruction or demolition of some barracks in the Main Camp area, the removal of a few guns from North Head positions, and the unusual activity of barges far out in Kiska Harbor. On 28 July, the Kiska radio lapsed into a silence which it has never subsequently broken. Photos taken in early August showed trucks parked on roads in the same position day after day, and no barges in Kiska Harbor or Gertrude Cove.

Naval shellings of Kiska installations during the first two weeks of August numbered twelve; no answering fire from enemy positions was received. Likewise with bombing missions returning from runs over Kiska—they reported light or no antiaircraft fire. When fire was reported, it was usually characterized as "small arms" fire.

The main body of Japanese troops on Kiska evacuated the island during the night of 28 July, either going by barge to waiting ships of the Fifth Fleet or to waiting submarines. By daylight 15 August, when United States and Canadian assault troops landed, even those small enemy detachments responsible for the small-arms fire reported by planes over Kiska after 28 July, were gone.

Thus ended Japan's brief hegemony in the Western Aleutians. Within a period of 14 months, the situation in the North Pacific had been reversed, and where a year ago Japan threatened our northern flank, we now threatened hers.

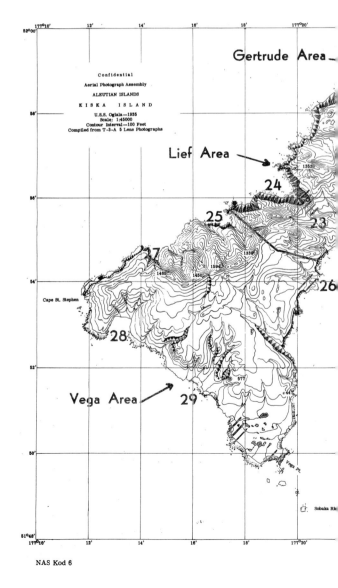

NAS Kod 6

-106-

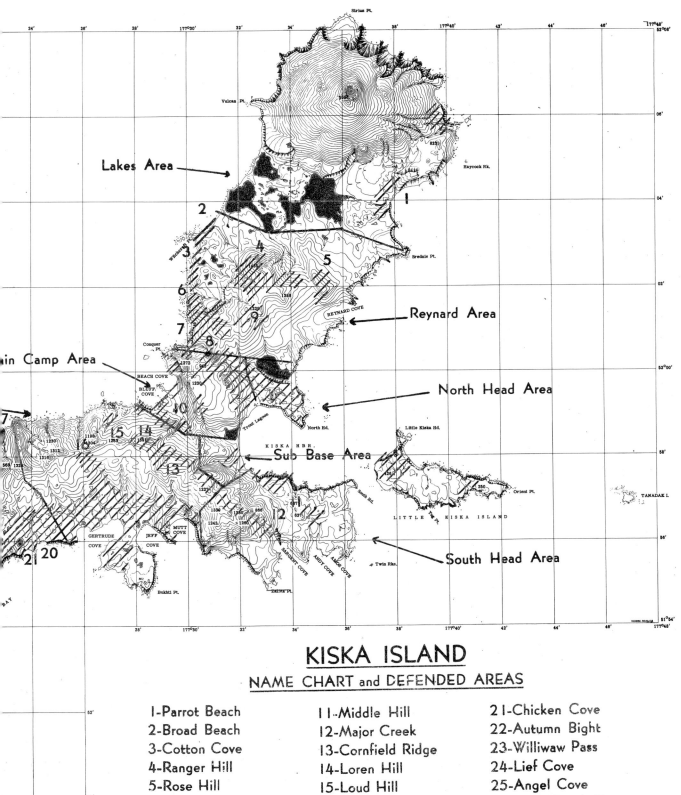

KISKA ISLAND

NAME CHART and DEFENDED AREAS

1-Parrot Beach	11-Middle Hill	21-Chicken Cove
2-Broad Beach	12-Major Creek	22-Autumn Bight
3-Cotton Cove	13-Cornfield Ridge	23-Williwaw Pass
4-Ranger Hill	14-Loren Hill	24-Lief Cove
5-Rose Hill	15-Loud Hill	25-Angel Cove
6-Wheat Cove	16-Link Hill	26-Tom Thumb Cove
7-Barley Cove	17-Quisling Cove	27-Devil Cove
8-Salmon Pass	18-Russian Ridge	28-Dark Cove
9-Riot Hill	19-Kidney Hill	29-Spring Cove
10-Middle Pass	20-Turkey Cove	30-Lilliput Cove

Cross hatching indicates defended areas.

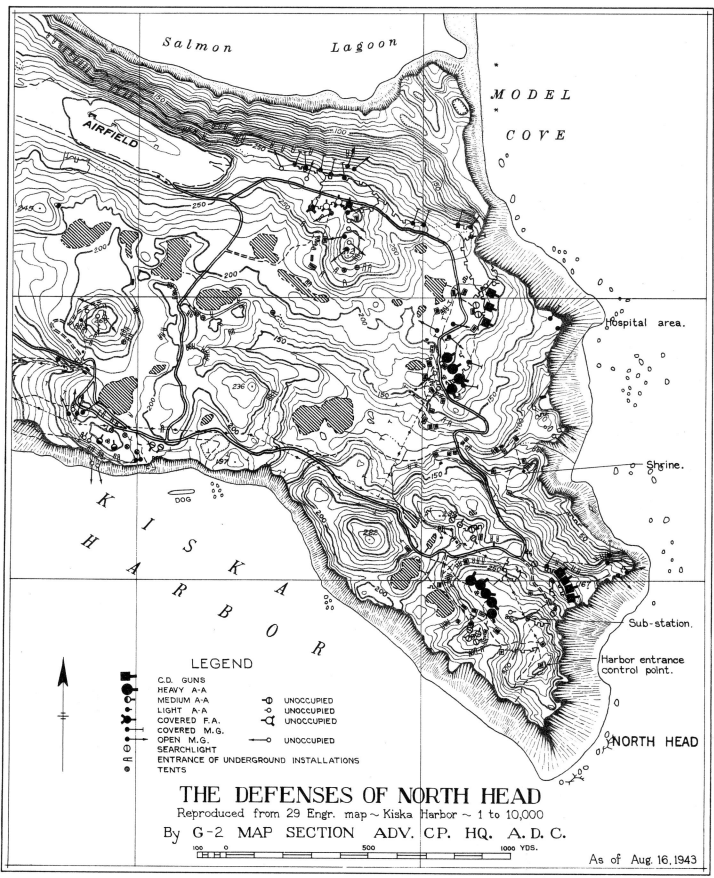

THE DEFENSES OF NORTH HEAD
Reproduced from 29 Engr. map ~ Kiska Harbor ~ 1 to 10,000

By G-2 MAP SECTION ADV. CP. HQ. A.D.C.

As of Aug. 16, 1943

The majority of the coastal and anti-aircraft guns were concentrated on North Head, which guarded the approach into Kiska Harbor. The location of the four dual purpose 120mm guns is marked in the circle in the upper part of the aerial photograph. The three 6-inch coastal defense guns, hidden by camouflage and not visible, were located directly north of the 120mm guns. The four 4.7-inch guns were sited on the bluff near the tip of the head to the south of the dual purpose guns. A battery of four 75mm dual purpose guns was located a short distance away to the west. In addition to these guns, Eleventh Air Force intelligence personnel noted two twin barrel 25mm, two single barrel 20mm, five 13mm twin barrel, four 13mm single barrel and 26-31 7.7mm guns on North Head. AAF

Japanese Strength on Kiska

Compiled by examining captured documents, the following units appear to have been on Kiska:

ARMY

301st Ind. Infantry Battalion (Could be Hokubu 4237 Unit, Bn. CO appears to be Major Hozumi Matsutoshi).

302nd Ind. Infantry Battalion (Hokubu 5212 Unit).

Ind. Engineers (No definite information has been found indicating the exact unit or strength, but it may be reasonably stated that a minimum of three platoons and a maximum of one company, one or two platoons of ship engineers was present. Part of the 6th Ship Engineer Regiment commanded by Colonel Muranaka).

2nd Co. of the 303rd Ind. Infantry Battalion (Could be Hokubu 5211. 2nd company of the 303rd, which was destroyed at Attu, appears to have been at Kiska).

32nd Antiaircraft unit.

22nd Antiaircraft Battery.

2nd Co. of the 301st Ind. Engineer Unit (2nd Co. believed to have been in Kiska, according to Prisoner of War information).

30th Constructed Field Hospital (There were two field hospitals with two majors in command. Majors Mochizuki and Yuhata, respectively). Nagamine Anchorage Unit.

Yasuda Mt. Artillery Ammunition Unit (Document with this information found on Little Kiska).

NAVY

51st Base Headquarters, CO, Rear Admiral Akiyama Katsuzo.

5th Defense Unit (This included the Maizuru 3rd Special Landing Party. As to whether it included the later landing party is not known. CO, Captain (Navy) Sato Toshio).

5th Defense Medical Unit.

AO Defense Unit (?).

2nd Regiment Special Garrison Troops.

Navigation Dept.

Meteorological Dept.

30th Billeting Unit (Evidently this unit was formed by civilians with the cadre being Navy personnel).

AIR UNITS

51st Base Air Unit (Probable commander was Commander Takahashi Nobukichi).

5th Air Unit (May have been a part of the 51st Base Air Unit).

Other units believed to have been on Kiska, but which have not appeared on the documents captured so far, are:

51st Communication Unit.
26th Submarine Unit.
Navy Antiaircraft Unit.
39th Stationary Wireless Unit.

Probable Location of Units:

An effort was made insofar as possible to determine the locality in which units were stationed; however, the only fairly positive identifications as to location follow:

GERTRUDE COVE	301st Ind. Inf. Bn.
KISKA HARBOR	51st Base Headquarters
	5th Defense Unit
	Navy Antiaircraft Unit
	26th Submarine Unit
	51st Base Air Unit
	5th Air Force
	30th Billeting Unit
	Navy Hospital
LITTLE KISKA	Yasuda Mt. Art. Amm. Unit

The total strength of enemy forces on Kiska was approximately 7,800.

TACTICAL STUDY OF THE TERRAIN

A. General Topography Of Area:

Kiska, together with the other western Aleutian Islands, is of volcanic origin and completely devoid of trees. Lying between the frigid Bering Sea and the more temperate Japanese current in the North Pacific Ocean, it is in that zone where weather is born and which is characterized by violent gales, heavy precipitation, long periods of fog, and rapid, unpredictable changes of temperature, barometric pressure, wind direction, wind velocity and cloudiness.

Kiska lies between latitude 51° 491′ 45″ north and 52° 08′ 18″ north; and longitude 177° 11′ 43″ east and 177° 40′ 25″ east. It has about the same latitude as London, England and the same longitude as New Zealand.

Running generally from northeast to southwest, Kiska is 25 miles long by eight miles wide at its widest part—a northwest-southeast line through South Head—land only 1.8 miles wide at its narrowest point—a northwest-southeast line through Lief Cove. Lying .6 mile from South Head is Little Kiska which extends east for four miles from this point, and averages 1.5 miles in width.

Kiska's shore line includes few beaches suitable for landing, the better of which were controlled by enemy fire, and generally consists of precipitous rocky cliffs bulwarked by reefs, pinnacle rocks, dangerous rip tides, and treacherous undertow. Normal surf to windward is seven feet high, and has been recorded at 35 feet during a blow.

The island in general ranges in height from 3,996 feet at the summit of the volcano to the north, through sea level lagoons and swamps at the volcano's foot, to a series of ridges averaging 1,200 feet.

Snow caps the volcano throughout most of the year, ranges down to cover the ridges for from six to eight months, reaches and remains at sea level for four months, from December to March inclusive.

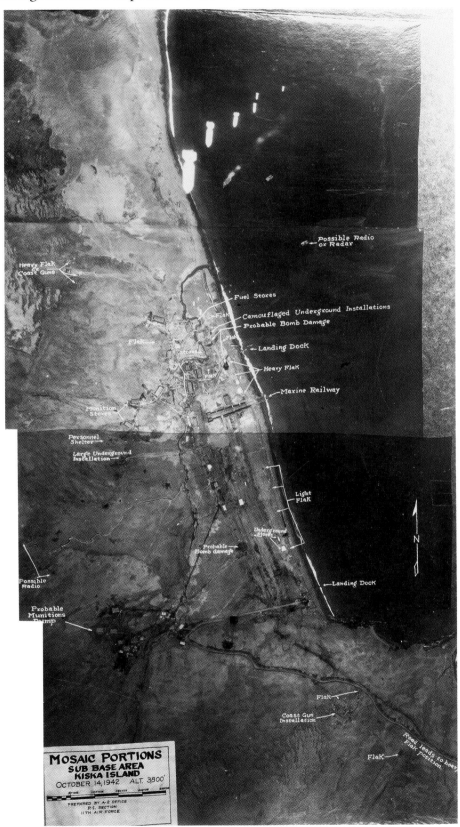

A mosaic of the sub-base area. USAF

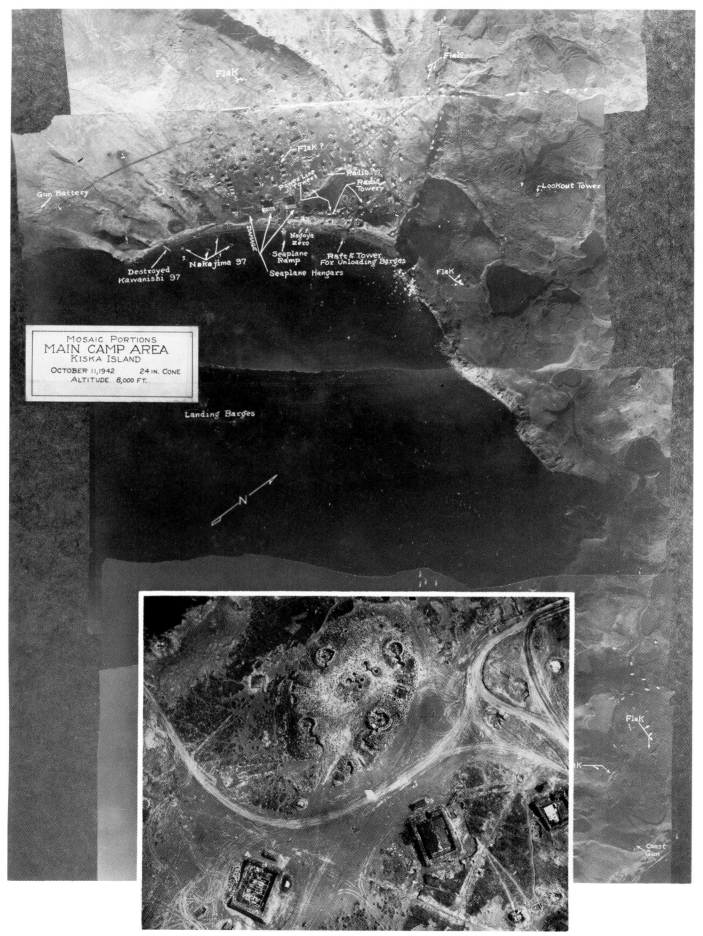

Aerial view of revetments. NA 80-G-83500-2

American cruisers bombard enemy installations on Kiska, Aug. 8, 1942. Shore batteries were silenced, fires started and severe damage was inflicted to the enemy camp areas. Photo taken from the *USS Wichita.* In the background are the *USS San Francisco* and *USS Louisville.*

Stern of the *Nashville* (CL43).

Bombs explode in the seaplane area of the main camp. USA

This series of photographs were taken during a low-level attack on the main camp at Kiska on Dec. 20, 1942. They illustrate how low the bombers had been flown on the Sept. 14 "max effort" raid. Until then, the bomber crews had flown their missions at high altitudes to avoid the light- and medium-altitude anti-aircraft fire. With the introduction of fighter escorts to suppress the Japanese anti-aircraft gunners, Colonel Eareckson's bomber crews began flying low-level missions as a matter of routine. USA

Aerial view of Kiska with Kiska Volcano in the background, June 10, 1943.

One of the more graphic pictures of the attacks against the runway was taken during a low-level mission. A bomb burst can be seen in the lower center near one of the several anti-aircraft positions located near the end of the runway and puffs from exploding flak are visible. The efforts made by the Japanese to build up the ends of the runway with fill is evident.

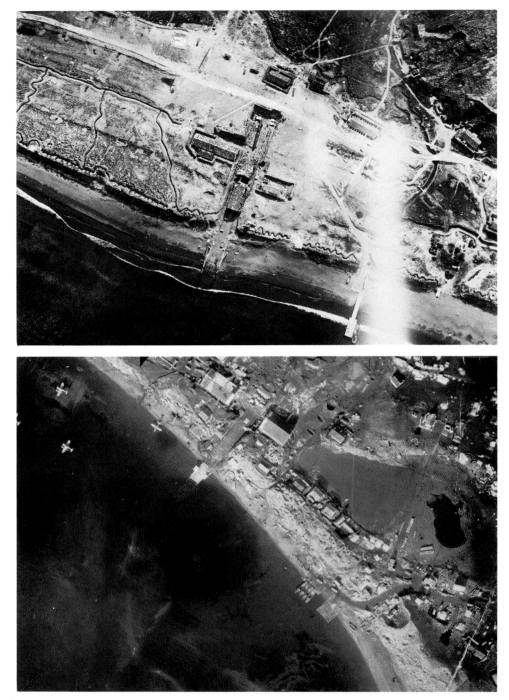

A closer view of the submarine shed and the marine rail way leading from it to the waters edge. The wavy lines were trenches. AAF

The seaplane base area at the main camp. The American weather station can be seen in the lower left-hand corner of the photograph. AAF

Kiska Defenses

The following report has been prepared to show the nature of Japanese defenses at Kiska and to describe types of enemy weapons, machinery, installations, and material. A previous report of 16 June 1943, ADV CP, Hq, ADC, describes installations found on Attu. All data presented here was gathered from ground reconnaissance during the period 17 August to 5 September by men and officers representing G-2 of the Alaska Defense Command and the Advanced Intelligence Center, North Pacific Area.

Although photo intelligence branches of both the Army and Navy had identified installations at Kiska with a high degree of accuracy before the operation, there were a few weapons which had not been encountered before about whose calibre and type there was some doubt. Considerable damage to buildings, to communication systems, and to guns by Japanese demolition charges and by the looting of troops limited the amount of useful intelligence derived from the Kiska installations. At the time of the Allied occupation only a few buildings remained undamaged by previous bombings and shellings; all guns had been rendered useless by damage to vital parts by the enemy; and nearly all mechanized equipment (including radio, radar, and motor transport) had been destroyed or rendered useless. Nevertheless, some worthwhile observations were possible.

The garrison at Kiska was different from any encountered thus far in this theater, in that it was composed of Army and Navy personnel in about equal numbers. Although a few Naval personnel were found at Attu, the garrison was composed almost entirely of Amy man and consequently the barracks, weapons, etc., were all of Army type. At Kiska the Navy was concentrated around Kiska Harbor, while the Army occupied the area around Gertrude Cove. Barracks and weapons of the Navy differed in some respect from those of the Army. In the future, particularly in the North Pacific Area, it is reasonable to expect installations similar to those on Kiska where both the Army and Navy occupied different sections of the same island.

Information obtained shows that the Japanese development of Kiska was much more extensive than the development of Attu. Almost all beaches possessed some defenses, including barbed wire and mines. In addition to the gun types found at Attu (75mm and 20mm AA; 75mm and 37mm Mtn. artillery; and small arms) Kiska ordnance included six inch, 4.7 inch,, and 76mm naval CD guns, 25mm and 13mm (single and twin mount) AA guns, and three light tanks. Heavy MGs were in a few cases mounted in concrete pill boxes. Passive defenses included a radar installation, two 150 cm searchlights, and two 98cm searchlights. Medical facilities were housed in well-equipped and underground hospitals.

In contrast to undeveloped Attu, Kiska defensive areas were linked by a fairly well-developed road network. Nearly 60 trucks, 8 sedans, 20 motorcycles, and 6 bantam-sized autos operated over this system. Two small bulldozers, tractors, and rollers were available for work on the Salmon Lagoon airfield. The submarine base with the remains of four small Sydney type subs, the sea plane base with the wrecks of probably forty fighter and reconnaissance float planes, two machine shops, a foundry, and a saw mill complete the list of Kiska's special installations.

Water and power system were well established at Kiska in contrast to rather primitive systems employed at Attu, the garrison was composed almost entirely of Army men and consequently the barracks, weapons, etc., special buildings and outlying areas. Water from half a dozen small reservoirs was piped to installations and fire hydrants throughout the Main Camp area. Three complete radio stations, a radio type navigation aid, and a well-installed telephone system made up the communication network.

KISKA GUN SUMMARY

Totals

Coast Defense Guns (Naval)
6 6"
4 4.7"
4 76mm
2 75mm

Antiaircraft
4 120mm—dual purpose
22 75mm—dual purpose
10 25mm—twin barrel
11 20mm
4 20mm—aircraft MG
14 13mm—twin barrel
4 13mm—single

Artillery
9 75mm Mtn guns
2 70mm howitzers
9 37mm Mtn guns

Machine Guns
20 (approx) 7.7 heavies
5 (approx) 7.7 lights
5 (approx) 6.5 Nambu lights
1 Lewis gun
(Parts for an estimated additional 20 heavies and 15 lights were observed. Still other MGs may have been evacuated with the Japanese garrison.)

Mortars
(Very few) 81mm
15 50mm, Model 89
1 50mm (new type)

Special
3 (light) tanks, armed with 1-37mm in turret and 1-MG in hull; M2595 (1935)
2 Wooden drill guns or dummies
2 Wooden dummy guns

MG Positions
150 (approx) Covered
100 (approx) open positions
(47mm ammunition was found but no guns of this caliber)

Geographic Breakdown

North Central Kiska
4 75mm AA guns
3 20mm AA guns
2 37mm Mtn artillery pieces
22 covered MG positions
30 open MG positions

North Head
- 3   6″ naval coast defense guns
- 4   4.7″ naval coast defense guns
- 4   120mm AA guns
- 4   75mm AA guns
- 2   25mm (twin mount) AA guns
- 2   20mm AA guns
- 5   13mm (twin mount) AA guns
- 4   13mm (single mount) AA guns and 4 positions with mounts only
- 2   75mm Mtn artillery pieces
- 1   wooden dummy or drill gun
- 15-20   covered MG positions (approx 10-7.7 guns and 5-6.5 Nambu guns observed)
- 11   open MG positions

Main Camp
- 2   76mm naval coast defense guns
- 4   75mm AA guns
- 8   25mm (twin mount) AA guns
- 5   20mm aircraft MG (stands only)
- 2   13mm (twin mount) AA guns
- 2   37mm Mtn artillery pieces
- 17   covered MG positions (parts of approx 10-7.7 and 5-6.5 MGs observed)
- 7   open MG positions
- 2   light tanks (1-37mm gun attached)

Sub Base
- 2   76mm naval coast defense guns
- 2   13mm (twin mount) AA guns
- 8   covered MG positions
- 2   open MG positions

South Head
- 4   75mm AA guns
- 4   20 aircraft MGs
- 4   covered MG positions
- 1   light tank (37mm gun; 2-7.7 guns attached)
- 1   wooden dummy or drill gun

Gertrude Cove
- 2   75mm coast defense guns
- 6   75mm AA guns
- 6   20mm AA guns
- 2   75mm Mtn artillery pieces (includes Ethel Cove)
- 3   37mm Mtn artillery pieces (includes Jeff and Ethel Coves)
- 16   covered MG positions (includes Jeff and Ethel Coves)
- 10   open MG positions (includes Jeff and Ethel Coves)
- 1   wooden dummy reported

Little Kiska
- 3   6″ naval coast defense guns
- 4   20mm aircraft MGs (positions and ammunition only)
- 5   (twin mount) AA guns
- 4   75mm Mtn artillery pieces
- 1   37mm Mtn artillery pieces
- 2   covered MG positions
- 1   open MG position

Beach and Bluff Coves
- 1   75mm Mtn artillery piece
- 1   37mm Artillery piece
- 20-23   covered MG positions
- 2-5   open MG positions

Vega Bay Shore
- 21   covered MG positions (1 wooden dummy gun)
- 19   open MG positions
- 2   70mm howitzers (Link Hill)

South Shore
- 8   covered MG positions

Southwest Shore
- 12   covered MG positions
- 4   open MG positions

Kiska invasion troops from California pass Alcatraz Island in San Francisco Bay, summer 1943. NA 111-SC-245188

Admiral Kinkaid, center, confers with other senior commanders during one of the planning sessions for retaking Kiska. To his immediate left are Generals Corlett, Buckner, Butler and G. R. Pearkes (Canada). To his right are Admiral Rockwell (head bowed) and General DeWitt. USA

The Kiska invasion fleet lies at anchor in an Alaska harbor awaiting the signal to steam toward the island. USNI

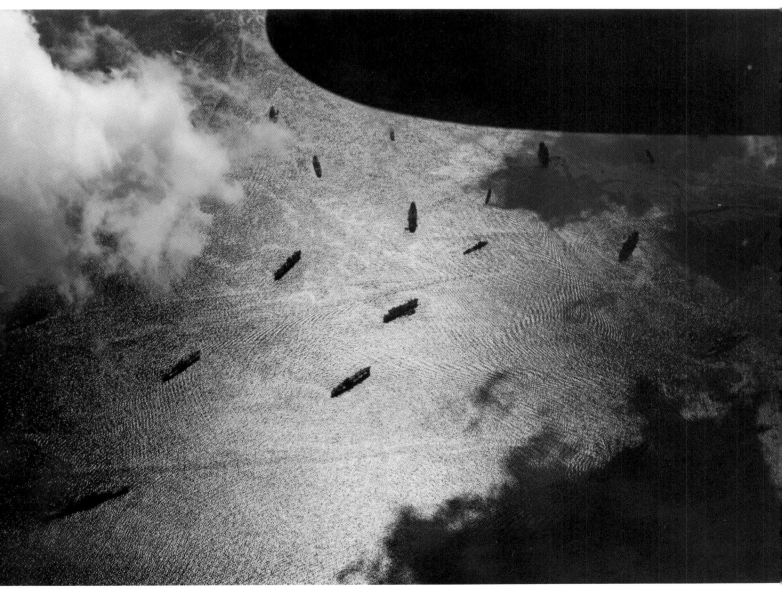

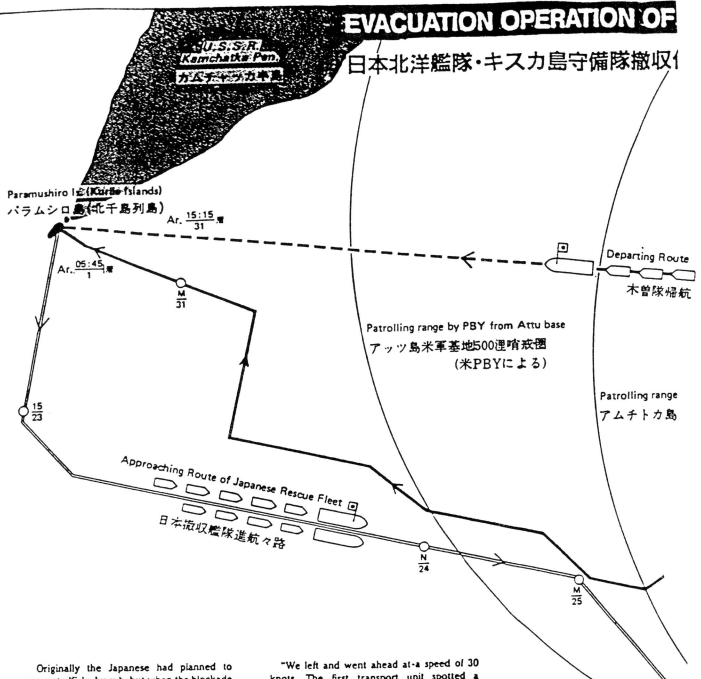

Originally the Japanese had planned to evacuate Kiska by sub, but when the blockade made that impossible they boldly dispatched 12 destroyers, newly equipped with radar and counter-radar equipment.

After an aborted attempt in early July, the Japanese fleet returned to Aleutian waters July 24 and played a game of cat and mouse with the American fleet until thick fog served as a cover July 29. Nervously they twice launched torpedoes at suspected enemy targets which turned out to be Little Kiska Island. The Americans were off refueling and replacing artillery spent earlier in an all-out attack on radar blips that have never been explained.

Two Japanese ships collided, putting one out of action and greatly limiting space for evacuees, but in 30 minutes over 5,000 Japanese soldiers managed to clamber aboard, the fleet upended anchor and made a dash for home.

"We left and went ahead at a speed of 30 knots. The first transport unit spotted a periscope northeast of Kiska, but the submarine immediately disappeared beneath the waves and thereafter wasn't seen again," a Japanese ensign recorded in his diary, captured later.

"At 0600 on the 31st the mist had completely cleared and at 1530 we entered Paramushiro Harbor. It seemed that heaven were celebrating our success..."

And, he gloated, it appeared the enemy had not discovered their evacuation.

"Thereafter, for day after day, they bombed and bombarded Kiska and on August 15, the landing of American and Canadian troops on that island was announced. Truly the height of the ridiculous."

Date and Time are based on "Japanese standard time". $\frac{7}{29}$ = at 7 o'clock on 29th, July. $\frac{N}{28}$ = at night on 28th. $\frac{M}{29}$ = at mid-night on 29th.

JAPANESE KISKA GARRISON (29 July~31 July, 1943.)

作戦図 （7月29日～31日、1943年）

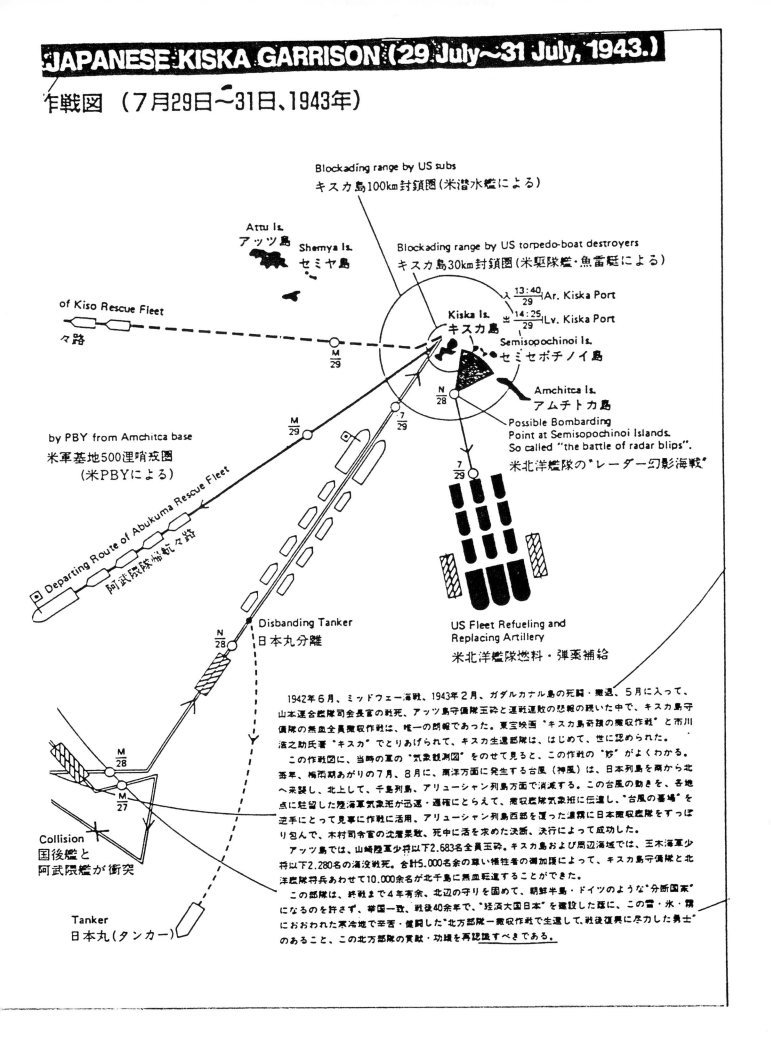

1942年6月、ミッドウェー海戦、1943年2月、ガダルカナル島の死闘・撤退、5月に入って、山本連合艦隊司令長官の戦死、アッツ島守備隊玉砕と連戦連敗の悲報の続いた中で、キスカ島守備隊の無血全員撤収作戦は、唯一の朗報であった。東宝映画 "キスカ島奇蹟の撤収作戦" と市川浜之助氏著 "キスカ" でとりあげられて、キスカ生還部隊は、はじめて、世に認められた。

この作戦図に、当時の軍の "気象観測図" をのせて見ると、この作戦の "妙" がよくわかる。毎年、梅雨期あがりの7月、8月に、南洋方面に発生する台風（神風）は、日本列島を南から北へ来襲し、北上して、千島列島、アリューシャン列島方面で消滅する。この台風の動きを、各地点に駐留した陸海軍気象兵が迅速・適確にとらえて、撤収艦隊気象班に伝達し、"台風の墓場" を逆手にとって見事に作戦に活用、アリューシャン列島西部を覆った濃霧に日本撤収艦隊をすっぽり包んで、木村司令官の沈着果敢、死中に活を求めた決断、決行によって成功した。

アッツ島では、山崎陸軍少将以下2,683名全員玉砕。キスカ島および周辺海域では、玉木海軍少将以下2,280名の海没戦死。合計5,000名余の尊い犠牲者の御加護によって、キスカ島守備隊と北洋艦隊将兵あわせて10,000余名が北千島に無血転進することができた。

この部隊は、終戦まで4年有余、北辺の守りを固めて、朝鮮半島・ドイツのような "分断国家" になるのを許さず、拳国一致、戦後40余年で、"経済大国日本" を建設する礎に、この雪・氷・霧におおわれた寒冷地で至苦・健闘し "北方部隊一撤収作戦で生還して、戦後復興に尽力した勇士" のあること、この北方部隊の貢献・功績を再認識すべきである。

The Multi-Hero of the Aleutians

by Joe Rychetnik

Bill Thies ate, slept and dreamed to be a Naval Aviator after he saw a Navy recruiter emerge from a neatly landed plane on the University of Maryland football field. The dress whites, the wings of gold and the way the pilot brought the plane in sold Thies and he rushed to join the Naval Aviation Cadet training program following his graduation with an engineering degree. He wanted to fly.

He spent six months learning the basics at New York's Floyd Bennett Naval Air Station where more than half the incoming class had dropped or been dropped out of the tough program. Ready for Pensacola, Thies stopped off at his home in Washington, D.C., long enough to get bit by the typhoid bug and instead of flying, he was fighting for his life for the next six months. He was a wreck when he came out of the sick bay and was told he could forget flight school; but he bucked the system and built himself up physically, passing the rigorous tests and examinations with flying colors.

Though Thies admitted everyone coming through Pensacola wanted to be a fighter pilot, he was a bit disappointed to be shuffled off to patrol bomber school to learn the business of flying a PBY, the Navy's twin engine long-range Consolidated Patrol Bomber.

From Pensacola Thies went to the altar, married (against existing regulation) his childhood sweetheart and they both drove his new roadster to his first duty station, Sand Point Naval Air Station, Seattle, where the young pilot would serve with VP-41 of Patrol Wing 4. There he was brought up to professional skill flying the PBYs from Seattle, Sitka and Kodiak. He was transferred to Kodiak just four weeks before Pearl Harbor and found himself out hunting the Japanese fleet two days later. He and a low-flying PBY (the other craft's engines would not keep the plane above 2,000 feet) thought they discovered the Japanese Fleet headed for Kodiak and radioed his base they had spotted a battlewagon and would attack, when close examination by the low-flying PBY revealed Thies was about to bomb a U.S. Navy cruiser. He had never seen one before!

He was then in a quandary as to how to report his error as the radio operator in Kodiak would not accept the message that the incoming Japanese fleet was now an American ship, suspecting a trick similar to Pearl Harbor. Over the radio the quiz began to perfectly identify Thies as an American pilot. Kodiak ran through a series of questions regarding American baseball teams and while the Marines and Army were shivering in their hastily dug slit trenches waiting for the Japanese invasion, Thies suggested his middle ini-

tial as an identifier since it was an unusual name. When he radioed that the "N" stood for "NOURIS," they accepted the report and stood down.

Flying long-range patrols in the PBY (some more than 12 hours long) over the stormy and often-foggy North Pacific made Thies an expert in handling the big slow craft. His crew of 10 got to be a tight family. When he was lost one time in heavy weather and running out of fuel, a momentary glimpse of the Shumagin Islands gave him the clue to finding his base at Dutch Harbor. While flying in over the Aleutian landscape an airsick crew member, heaving his guts out of the port waist machine gun bubble, saw just below the plane an upside down Zero fighter. Thies made a circle and spotted the mystery plane on his chart of Akutan Island and later nearly ended his career by demanding the Navy recover the plane. He wanted to lead the recovery crew, which he finally did.

The discovery of the Akutan Zero gave the U.S. military and naval aviation an advantage over the Japanese, who rated their Zero fighter one of their most effective war machines. It had proven vastly superior against anything the Allies could put up to it from the P-40s to the Navy's Brewster Buffalo and Grumman Wildcat. With the Zero repaired and flown by Navy test pilots, Army Air Corps aero-engineers, and experts such as Charles Lindbergh, the United States was able to design tactics against the Zero and eventually launch aircraft which were far superior to the Zero, such as the F6F Hellcat, the F4U Corsair, the Lockheed P-38 and finally the P-51 Mustang.

Thies feels his insistence on recovering the Zero wreck was his most important asset in the war. He doesn't count as well that he later bombed the Japanese fleet invading Kiska and because of low clouds, fog and flak, turned his lumbering PBY 100 mph bomber into a Stuka dive bomber, sinking an enemy transport at Kiska and putting into the icy water perhaps a thousand or more enemy soldiers. For that repeated effort at Kiska he was awarded the Navy Cross by SEC-NAV Frank Knox in a chow hall ceremony at Dutch Harbor.

Thies was eventually rotated back to the States to prepare for taking over as Executive Officer of a Navy PV Harpoon squadron on Whidbey Island. Just before he was to leave for the war in the southwest Pacific he was talked into leading, but probably volunteered, a radio team onto the beaches of soon to be invaded Kiska Island, his old "stomping ground." He would be taken to the Aleutians in an Army transport with the American forces.

"The Navy felt I was the most qualified man to

lead a recon force onto Kiska as I had flown it so many times," Thies said. "I knew I was well out of my element once aboard the Army transport and now told to gear up for the landing. We had never been taught about small arms firing but before I went over the side of that transport I was handed a carbine, had a .45 auto strapped on with plenty of ammo, and had a bunch of grenades fastened to my jacket. The radio was on a jeep and the jeep was loaded into a landing craft with the Army crew. It remained for me to decide when and where we would go in with the radio and set up our observation post.

"There was a big bombardment by Adm. Kinkaid's ships. He had claimed he had a ring of steel around the island and that he would kill most of the Japanese with his naval guns. There were reports from various intelligence sources that the code had been broken and that the enemy had left Kiska but Kinkaid was determined to prove his "ring of steel" had contained the Japanese and now his big guns would demolish them. They had, of course, fled the island two weeks before.

"The fleet anchored on the west side of the island and Canadian Army troops on the other side didn't know the enemy was gone. The two armies met and clashed and several were killed before it was known they were shooting at each other. We were listening on the ship's radio to the reports of a fierce mortar battle and we knew we would have to land elsewhere to set up a post.

"The Army's plan was to get a secure beachhead and then we would land our jeep there and start calling in aircraft to assist the Army. We had Army airfields all around Kiska—on Attu, Amchitka, at Dutch Harbor and elsewhere, ready to go. My party was made up of 10 Army men—the radio operators, jeep drivers and a small detail of riflemen to keep us secure. What really scared me after the reports of the mortar battle, was the fact that a nearby destroyer, about 550 yards off from the transport, I think it was the *Abner Reid*, had struck a Japanese mine with her stern and blew up, showering debris and men all over us. I didn't know whether to go down to the bouncing landing craft or get back on the ship but went down and we headed for the island, looking for a quiet place to land.

"We headed for the beach and I directed the barge around a point to where we could see some buildings and supplies piled up. There was no shooting here and we rolled ashore. I had all these guns and grenades which I had no idea how to use and was relieved to learn from a GI that popped out of the dawn that, 'The Japanese were all gone.'

"Our radio crew got the radio going and I was speaking directly to the admiral's staff out at sea. Of course, other bases could read me as well. I told them the enemy was gone. It was the first official word released that the Japanese had fled in the nights preceding the invasion. The only Japanese we could find were dead ones. The whole invasion and shooting and waste of our soldiers' and Canadian soldiers' lives was unnecessary."

Thies was shipped to Sitka where he caught a PBY flight to Kodiak. He reported to Capt. Gehres, who still commanded the Patrol Wing and asked if there was any way he could fly back "to the States," as he hated the troop transport and there was nothing else heading south. Gehres told him that all he had at Kodiak was a broken down Lockheed Ventura patrol bomber that would fly but "that was about all it could do." The radios and most of the navigational equipment were not working.

Thies checked the plane and said he would fly it to Whidbey Island. Gehres offered him 15 Navy men who wanted to get back for various reasons. They took off one morning with a full load of fuel and some charts and hoped to make Annette Island, near Ketchikan for refueling. Fog prevented Thies from finding Annette so he opted to fly all the way to Whidbey with what fuel he had on board. He then hit a storm over the British Columbia coast and had to fly down on the deck, more or less blind.

"I had a rough idea where I was but no radio or radio direction finder to take bearings. I just sat there hoping something would open up and when I could stand it no longer I turned the plane due east and hoped for a landfall. There was nothing but fog and I expected to either hit the mountains on Vancouver Island or the Olympics on the Olympic Peninsula. All I could see was water less than 20 feet below us. It was then I prayed for the first time in my life. I asked the Lord for guidance and at that moment, for only 10 seconds, the sun gleamed on Neah Bay lighthouse off to our starboard and then it was thick fog again. I knew where I was and 15 minutes later we were over Whidbey in bright sunlight.

"When we landed (and they had not had any notice we were coming in as I had no radio) we were followed by the crash trucks and fire wagons. When we stopped they shouted for us to leave the plane running as we were leaking a lot of gas. I couldn't figure that as we still showed some gas in the tanks but I ran anyway. When nothing happened, I went back to the plane and checked the "gas" on the deck and found it to be seawater. We had flown so low and for so long that our prop wash was flooding the bomb bay with water. Must have been at least a barrel of water that came out when we landed."

Thies finally got his Harpoon Patrol Squadron command on Saipan and was stationed on Tinian Island, when the A-bomb was dropped. After postwar schooling, and serving as an exec on the Korean War supply ship *Jupiter*, Thies served in the Pentagon and retired as a captain. Now retired, he is a conservationist and steelhead fisherman.

Thies made the cover of the November 1942 issue of *Alaska Life* magazine.

Bill Thies in retirement at Carmel, Calif. JOE RYCHETNIK

Troops loading on transports at Adak for the Kiska invasion. FDR LIBRARY

Part of the Kiska invasion fleet in Adak Harbor, July 30, 1943. NA 111-SC-245189

Boarding an LCM at Adaka to be taken to the ships in the harbor. NA 80-G-42805

On board the USS *Harris* (APA-2) practicing abandoned ship drills. NA 80-G-10376

Maj. Gen. Charles Corlett and Brig. Gen. Joseph Ready reviewing troops at Fort Ord, California, May 15, 1943, prior to going to Kiska. USA SC-176671

Kiska bound troops on board ship examine two types of grenades. Notice that the trooper on the right has his Kiska patch pinned on his sleeve, not sewn on. Some men wore only one such patch, some had a patch on both shoulders. NA 80-G-103738

Loading equipment on a transport ship at Adak for the Kiska invasion. NA 80-G-103686

Party on board a Kiska-bound ship the night before the invasion. Lt. Col. Arthur Henderson cuts a cake. NA 111-SC-325816

Landing craft on the beach at the Japanese submarine base. Parts of several midget submarines lie on the beach. One of these pieces is still in the same position today. 11TH AIR FORCE

Members of the 87th Mountain Infantry Regiment unload supplies at the southern sector command post. DENVER PUBLIC LIBRARY HISTORY DEPT.

Men and equipment of the 87th Mountain Infantry Regiment unloading supplies on Lilly Beach, August 16. DENVER PUBLIC LIBRARY HISTORY DEPT.

Men and equipment on Blue
Beach. KANSAS STATE
HISTORICAL SOCIETY

Amphibious tractors lined up
at Trout Lagoon. The
Nozima Maru, part of which
is still in place, is to the right.
ASL US ARMY SIGNAL CORPS

Troops loading into landing boats for the Kiska invasion.
NA 80-G-103752.

Soldiers hunt for their barracks bags through piles stacked on the beach.
USA SC-182870

First Casualties on D-Day, Lilly Beach.
NA 80-G-55672

On the beach. NA 111-SC-337842

D-Day, Quisling Cove. NA 80-G-78473

Landing barges traveled to the beach in pairs in the event of mishap on the reef and rock strewn approaches to Kiska. One could rescue the men aboard the other if necessary. USNI

Three types of landing craft on Lilly Beach loading trailers. Some men are working, some are just lounging on the rocks and rubber boats. USNI

Every man had a job to do upon reaching the beach. Here troops are loading one of the specially designed tractor trailers. A ramp was quickly built out into the water to facilitate easy unloading of the barges. USNI

Bow doors of two LSTs that have discharged their cargoes at the landing beach. The opening bow doors of the LST (Landing Ship, Tanks) were the most revolutionary development in amphibious operations in the war. Coast Guardsmen usually named these ships. US COAST GUARD

LCTs and LCMs and LCPs at the northwest landing beach on D-Day, August 15. Troops swam ashore and up the hillside with much equipment already on shore. At this time it was not known that the enemy had already evacuated the island. USNI

These troops walk off their LCM on the rocky shores of Kiska ready to face an enemy who was not there. Note that a censor has scratched out the Kiska patch on the soldier's shoulders. USNI

Troops head out over the rocky beach to their objective inland. USNI

Climbing in the tundra and high grass was exhausting to the troops. NA 80-G-103783

Troops haul a field gun up a hillside above the landing area at Quisling Cove. USNI

Soldiers set up a pyramidal tent as the wind blows, very typical for this isolated island in the Aleutian Chain.
USA SC-325823

A massive American supply and fuel dump with dozens of pyramidal tents in the background, Sept. 7, 1943.
USA SC-237843

The American flag is raised on a captured bunker ending 13 months of Japanese occupation. USNI & NA 111-SC-571608

Canadian troops on Kiska. KHS

Using a sharpened bayonet and shovel, two servicemen make kindling for their cooking fire on the second day of the island's occupation. USNI

American Red Cross Field Director Mat Howard serves at the first "Snack Bar" installed on Kiska after the invasion force landed. The "bar" was made of plain planks and empty oil drums but it was as magnificent as any bar anywhere to the troops on the beach as they drank their hot coffee in the lea of a Japanese seaplane hangar.
AMERICAN RED CROSS

A GI holds the dog Explosion, the pet of the U.S. Navy Weather Detachment which was captured on Kiska. Explosion endured 13 months of Japanese occupation and greeted the Allied troops as they landed on the island. USNI

A soldier dug into the tundra ready for the enemy, who had fled two weeks before the Allied landing. NA 80-G-103768

Death or serious injury lay ahead for anyone foolhardy enough to disregard this sign. It was erected by sappers assigned the ticklish task of removing the "booby traps" sown by the departing Japanese. USNI

Members of the Royal Canadian Army read about the action on Kiska, in *Yank* Magazine, September 1943.
NA 111-SC-325841

Allied troops overlooking a landing beach area.
NA 80-G-103771

A. G.I. is aiming a Japanese T. 96 Nambu, with no magazine. NA

Living conditions shortly after the occupation in mostly wet high grass on the tundra were anything but comfortable. USA SC-325825

Inside an abandoned Japanese hospital. USNI

A funeral procession for four Canadian soldiers to be buried in the New Canadian Cemetery, Oct. 15, 1943.
USA SC-236715

American and Canadian graveyard, Nov. 5, 1943. USA SC-236583

Remains of the sub-base showing the three midget subs still intact. The sub in the foreground is still in its original position today. NA 111-SC-189261

The submarine ramp and repair shop with a midget submarine cradled in the foreground. USA SC-182860

In this view the two subs in the background have been moved and debris has been removed from the site. Tents have been pitched around the area. 11TH AIR FORCE

Midget (Type A) Sub Base

The sub-base facilities consisted of a marine railway, a machine and battery repair shop, a marine equipment storage building, an acid storage building and a power house. The marine railway was made up of two sets of tracks (6'), which ran from the water to the long, high roofed sub shed that sheltered the subs while being repaired. The subs were moved over the railway on steel cradles, which were hauled out of the water by means of two large winches installed at the shore end of the base. Four subs, damaged by both American bombing and Japanese demolition were found. The subs measured just under 80 feet long and were powered by storage batteries. Two 45cm torpedoes were carried in bow tubes set in the hull.

The author stands beside the only intact midget sub still on the island. Only three others are known to exist: one on Guam, one at Japan's Naval Academy and the sub captured at Pearl Harbor, now on display at the Admiral Nimitz Museum in Fredericksburg, Texas.

The rear propeller of the midget sub is still well preserved.
DONALD McARTHUR

Reproduction by Detachment 29th Engineers stationed with Hq, W.D.C. & Fourth Army, 1943   PLATE NO 4   SUB BASE   Drawn from photographs by Pvt John P Wheat
8th AAF Photo Intelligence Detachment, Hq Fourth AAF

6" Coast Defense Gun

Altogether there were six 6" CD guns at Kiska—three on North Head and three on Little Kiska. Some of these were of Japanese manufacture; others were of British make. Two guns on North Head were made by the Kure Naval Arsenal and one by Armstrong Whitworth and Co., Ltd. (Model 1900). Similarly, on Little Kiska, two guns were manufactured by the Kure Naval Arsenal and one by Sir Armstrong Mitchell (Model 1894). One gun on Little Kiska had been hit many times by 50-caliber aircraft machine gun bullets, but none of these had penetrated the shield. All guns were mounted on heavy steel spiders set directly in the soil with no concrete base. The North Head battery possessed two three-meter range finders, and both batteries had typical fire control centers placed behind the guns in small covered buildings. A few of the guns of Japanese manufacture were rifled with 28 lands in contrast to the British guns which had 48 lands. Except for this peculiarity, however, there was little difference between the two makes. The recoil mechanisms of the guns contained recuperator tubes similar to those on our ordnance of corresponding caliber. Camouflage nets had been stretched over a few of the North Head gun revetments, but this deception was ineffective.

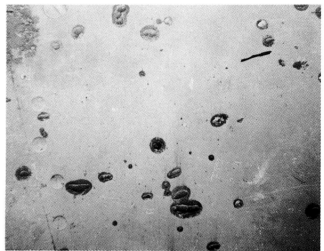

	CHARACTERISTICS
Type:	Navy
Bore:	6"
Barrel:	20' overall; 12' from shield to muzzle
Traverse:	360 degrees
Elevation:	30 degrees (approximate)
Breech:	Interrupted screw
Weight:	14,784 lbs.
Shield:	1¼" plate on sides; 4" plate on front; 2 ½" plate on top
Revetments:	26' inside diameter
Ammunition:	Semi-fixed—powder charge of one increment. (Separate primers were found which screwed into the cartridge case after a plug placed there for shipping purposes had been removed.)

Today the 6″ guns on Little Kiska Island seem to be ready to fire again. The three guns on Little Kiska are in much better condition than those on North Head.

120mm Dual-purpose Gun

120 MM. DUAL PURPOSE

CHARACTERISTICS

Type:	Naval (pedestal mounts set in concrete)
Bore:	120 mm
Barrel:	45 caliber
Traverse:	360 degrees
Elevation:	75 degrees
Breech:	Sliding wedge
Shield:	⅜″ plate—splinter-proof only—open at rear
Revetment:	22′ inside diameter
Weight:	2910 kilograms

13mm AA Gun

13 MM. A-A GUN

The Japanese (Model 1942) 13mm AA gun is an air-cooled weapon that corresponds in most respects with our 50-caliber machine gun. Mounted both singly and as duals these guns were used at Kiska for anti-aircraft defenses. Most Kiska 13mm guns were manufactured at the Toyokawa Naval Factory. Revetments for the guns varied in diameter from 8 to 10 feet. Ammunition was ball, AP and tracer loaded 4 ball, 1 tracer, 4 AP.

A 13mm AA gun on North Head.

20mm AA Gun

The 20mm AA gun, also used at Attu, is a rapid fire automatic weapon that shoots both AP and HE shells, usually in the ratio of one to one. The 20mm gun barrel, about seven feet long with two recuperators underneath the tube, is mounted on a base of three spider legs, which may be put on wheels for traveling. At Kiska 20mm positions were set up individually and in battery usually to support the fire of larger 75mm batteries. Revetments for these guns measured from 8 to 10 feet in diameter.

The bottom right photo shows a one-of-a-kind weapon taken out of a plane and mounted on a U.S. bomb casing. The grips are homemade.

20 MM. A·A GUN

75 MM. DUAL PURPOSE A-A

Dual-purpose 75mm guns were the predominant type of ordnance used at Kiska. A total of 22 such guns were found set up in batteries located in all of the strategic Kiska areas. Usually these guns were established in a four-gun battery, sometimes in the shape of an "L," with fire control instruments located at the center. Fire control instruments consisted of three-meter height finders, 3-5 10cm binoculars (per battery), data computers, and covered CP buildings. Communication between guns and CPs was provided by speaking tubes and by buzzer systems. Individual guns had a 360-degree traverse, an 85-degree elevation, a 44.5-caliber barrel, and were set up on five spider legs that fold in when the gun is in traveling position. Guns had no shields but were sunk about five feet below the top of their revetments, which measured 18 to 20 feet in diameter. All guns were camouflaged by yellow, green, and brown paint. Ammunition was semi-fixed with 30-second time fuses, shell Model 90 and fuse Model 89.

These photos show a 4.7-inch gun.

The 25mm AA gun found on Kiska had not been encountered before in the Aleutian theater, although ammunition for it had been found on the beach at Attu, possibly awaiting trans-shipment to Kiska. All guns of this type on Kiska were dual-barreled Naval guns; but in the South Pacific area similar guns have been found fitted with three barrels. The gun is a rapid fire, air-cooled weapon highly effective against low-flying aircraft. Its magazine holds 15 shells with the ratio of one tracer to four HE, and its ammunition has a large propelling charge that gives the weapon a high muzzle velocity. The 25mm projectile has three rotating bands, two on the portion of the shell which lies outside the brass case. Projectiles also are fitted with point detonating fuses and with bursting charges of tetrel. Revetments for 25mm AA guns measure approximately 15 feet in diameter. Command posts in the form of prefabricated steel-plated turrets were emplaced in the ground near two of the 25mm positions.

25 MM. A-A GUN

4.7" Coast Defense Gun

4.7" C.D. GUN

Four 4.7" CD guns, two manufactured by the Kure Naval Arsenal and two by Armstrong Whitworth and Co. (Model 1905), were emplaced in a battery located near the tip of North Head. Except for size and for the lack of shields and bicycle traversing gear, these guns correspond in most respects with the 6" CD guns. Telephone and buzzer systems connected the guns with a fire control center, a three-meter range finder, and probably with the two 150 cm searchlights located adjacent to the battery. Firing was accomplished by an electrical trigger mechanism operated by the gunner. More camouflage was used on these guns than on the North Head 6" battery, but here, too, it provided little concealment.

CHARACTERISTICS

Type:	Navy (pedestal mount set in concrete)
Bore:	4.7"
Barrel:	16.5'
Traverse:	360 degrees
Elevation:	30 degrees (approx.)
Breech:	Interrupted screw
Shield:	None
Revetment:	20' inside diameter
Ammunition:	Semi-fixed; one increment of powder in raw silk bag inside brass shell case.

THREE METER RANGE FINDER 4.7" C.D BATTERY

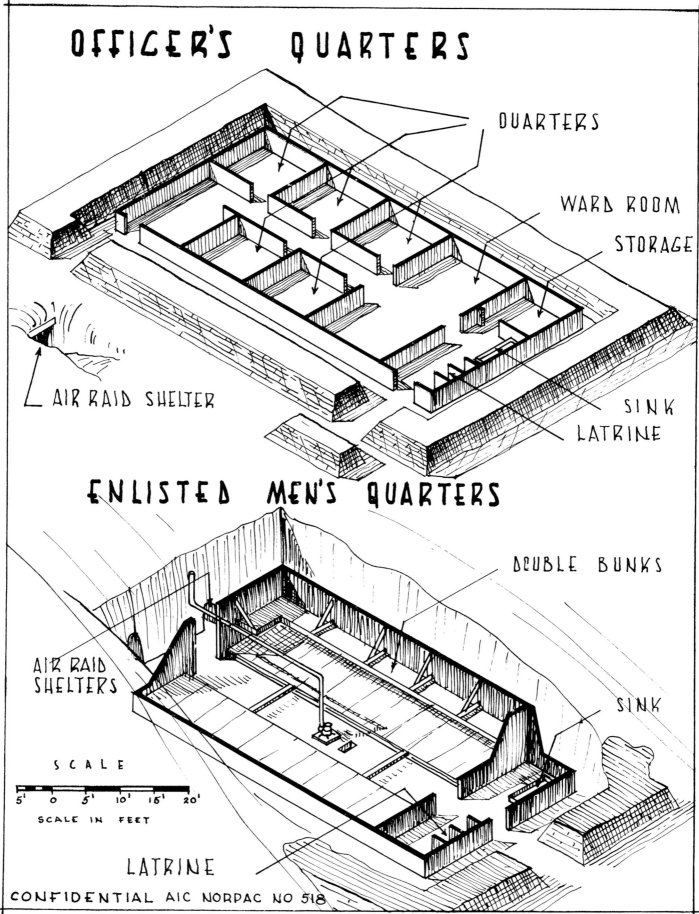

OFFICER'S QUARTERS

QUARTERS

WARD ROOM

STORAGE

AIR RAID SHELTER

SINK

LATRINE

ENLISTED MEN'S QUARTERS

DOUBLE BUNKS

AIR RAID SHELTERS

SINK

SCALE

5' 0 5' 10' 15' 20'

SCALE IN FEET

LATRINE

CONFIDENTIAL AIC NORPAC NO 518

NAS Adak 140

Japanese building, possibly a barracks, partially destroyed by Allied bombing. UNI

PLATE NO. 3   MAIN CAMP. TYPICAL JAP CONSTRUCTION—
BUILDINGS DUG INTO BASE OF HILL.

"SOUTH CAMP" UNDERGROUND HOSPITAL

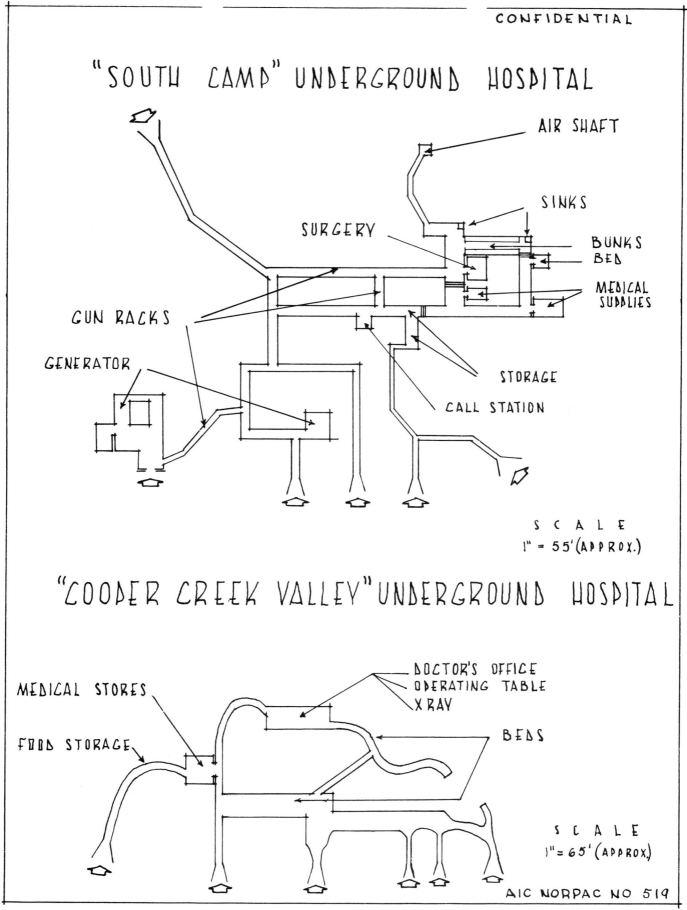

AIR SHAFT

SINKS

SURGERY

BUNKS
BED

GUN RACKS

MEDICAL
SUPPLIES

GENERATOR

STORAGE

CALL STATION

SCALE
1" = 55'(APPROX.)

"COOPER CREEK VALLEY" UNDERGROUND HOSPITAL

MEDICAL STORES

DOCTOR'S OFFICE
OPERATING TABLE
X RAY

FOOD STORAGE

BEDS

SCALE
1" = 65'(APPROX.)

AIC NORPAC NO 519

NAS Adak 141

-154-

The fighter strip on Kiska, constructed by the Japanese but not finished before they evacuated the island.

USA 80-G-157940 & AMHA & USAF

A Japanese victory garden in front of a gun emplacement at North Head. USA SC-272539

Coast Guardsman Harvey Gilbert, Seaman first class, of Philadelphia, Pennsylvania, astride a Japanese bicycle on the deck of a Coast Guard-manned LST (Landing Ship Tanks) following the reoccupation of Kiska. USNI

Gaping hole in the hull of the Japanese ship, *Nozima Maru*, which is beached at Kiska today. USNI

Interior of a seaplane hangar with many destroyed enemy float planes. USNI

Wrecked Japanese airplanes, oil and gas drums overlooking Kiska harbor. USAF

Demolished Japanese seaplanes on the beach. USA SC-337843 and USNI

Captured Japanese flags.

This flag indicates a Rear Admiral, and the only rear admiral evacuated from Kiska was Adm. Katsuzo Akiyama the ranking naval officer on the island. Note the British Bren-gun on the ground.

Snow completely covers the supply room of the 762nd Aircraft Warning Company, Jan. 4, 1944. USA SC-236499

Ordnance yards showing "snow" jeeps gathered together, Jan. 4, 1944. USA SC-236506

Regimental area of the 87th Mountain Infantry Regiment taken from Co. A, 1st Battalion area, Oct. 25, 1943. DPL

Hundreds of tents and Quonset huts were built to house the thousands of troops that occupied Kiska in the summer of 1943.
ASL, JAMES SIMPSON MACKINNON COLL.

Marston mat was placed on the ground leading down to the harbor as a possible beaching area for seaplanes.
ASL, JAMES SIMPSON MACKINNON COLL.

INTERIOR OF JAP NAVY BARRACKS

A Navy-built frame building constructed of prefabricated panels and triangular trusses. The buildings were protected by high blast walls. While the Army-built buildings were emplaced deep in the ground, the Navy-type were built on top of the ground.

TUNNEL AT HOSPITAL, MAIN CAMP

UNDERGROUND HOSPITAL, CAMP AREA

Hospital facilities on Kiska were built underground and were well developed. Tunnels connected several of these units, which were well stocked and some rooms were found in good condition.

Four searchlights were found—two 150cm and two 98cm, all were broken up by the Japanese.

Gasoline generator.

A lot of Japanese construction equipment was left on the island.

A total of about 60 Nissan trucks were found. Most were four-wheel, two-wheel drive; but a few were six-wheel, four-wheel drive. Also found were two tank trucks, two fire trucks, a water purification unit truck, and one truck with a mounted air compressor. One truck was found on Little Kiska with a built-in 98cm searchlight.

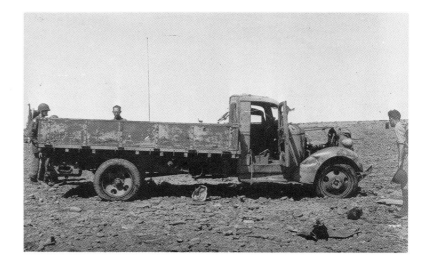

JAPANESE MOTORCYCLE & CONCRETE MIXER

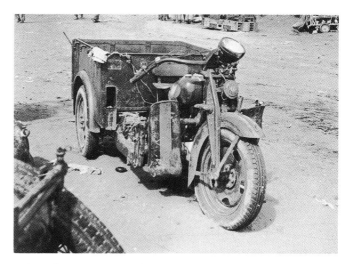

A total of 18 motorcycles were found in various conditions. Some were easily repaired and put into use. Eleven were similar to Harley Davidsons, of these seven had sidecars. The remaining seven were of the three-wheeled delivery type. On the left is a Rikuo motorcycle and on the right, a Mazda.

Six small Kurogane four-wheel drive scout cars were on the island, similar to a Bantam or Crosley, powered by a two-cylinder, air-cooled motorcycle engine. Eight sedans were found, six Nissans and two 1937 Fords.

DATSUN MOTOR CAR

The radio navigation aid was set up in the form of a V-shaped antenna that put out a signal on a 60 MC frequency. An improvised device that measured 20 feet on a side, it was used to help guide ships into the harbor.

A radar facility was found to the west of the Main Camp area on a hill 500 feet above sea level. It consisted of two screens that had a 360-degree traverse, which was moved by hand or motor. The facility had a 100 MC frequency and was of limited range.

Sawmill, Main Camp area.

An armored command post sunk in the tundra.

A total of six steamrollers were found, all powered by four-cylinder gasoline motors.

Two lightly constructed bulldozers, not well suited for heavy construction work, were found near the Salmon Lagoon airfield.

Three of these Model 1935 light tanks were found. All were used for beach defenses. One was buried in the beach bluff at Main Camp with just its gun turret above ground, and another had been burned out. The third was in good condition, emplaced in a revetment near Elephant Hill.

A Japanese 50mm mortar and projectile.

One Japanese fire hydrant is
still in place on the island.

A Japanese Shinto Shrine just up from the beach area. The
archway has been in place since 1942.

Remains of a possible
Japanese barracks.

This Japanese motorcycle is slowly sinking into the tundra.

Many remains of Japanese Nissan trucks have been collected in a large scrap pile.

A U.S. Army tractor, one of many that were used on the island to transport personnel and supplies.

An outdoor Japanese oven with large openings for pots. Was it used for cooking or heating water for bathing?

A piece of equipment, possibly a winch on Little Kiska Island. Hundreds of .50 caliber shells are lying around the site; who left them or why they are there has not been determined.

Remains of a cairn dedicated on Oct. 10, 1943, by the 24th Field Regiment, Royal Canadian Artillery, who were stationed on Kiska. This is the same cairn as pictured on page 176.

A 37mm M-94 anti-tank gun on Little Kiska Island appears to be in good condition. A complete four-gun battery was in place on the island during the Japanese occupation. This highly mobile gun type was also used in the battle for Attu.

A metal box filled with Japanese anti–aircraft ammunition lies on the tundra on Little Kiska Island.

Remains of a Japanese truck on Little Kiska Island.

A Japanese Zero engine in the scrap yard.

Assorted "junk," possibly both Japanese and American, in a scrap yard just up from the beach.

Several members of the 87th Mountain Infantry Regiment made a pilgrimage back to Kiska in 1983 to place this plaque as a memorial to their comrades. EARL CLARK

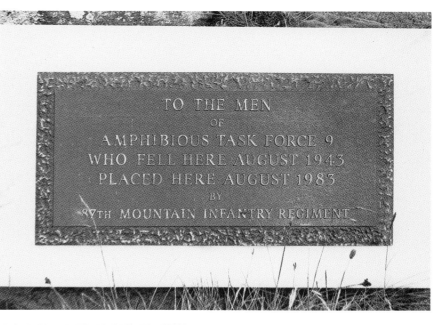

Remains of the roadway leading to the dock in Kiska Harbor, built by the U.S. Army after the occupation of the island.

These two water tanks on a hill above the harbor were built by the U.S. Army during their stay on the island. These structures, one Quonset hut, some overgrown roads, many telephone poles, and the dock are the last vestiges of the American occupation still in place.

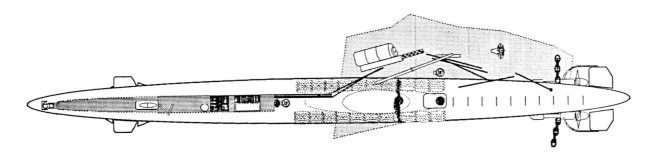

RO-65

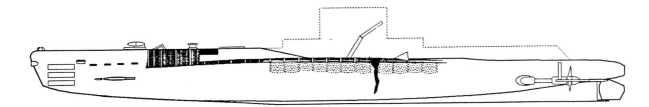

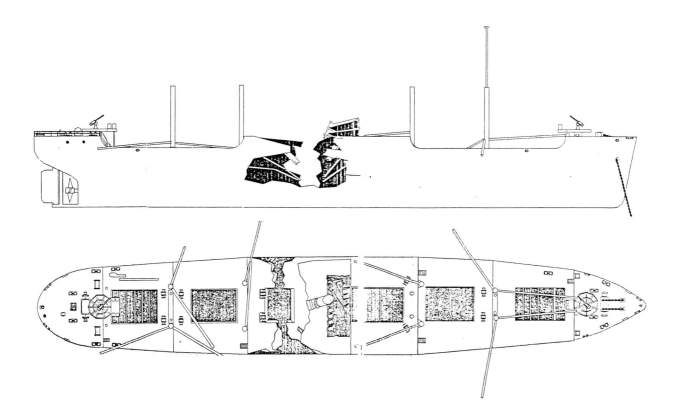

During September 1989, the National Park Service with the cooperation of the U.S. Third Fleet conducted project Seamark to locate and document submerged objects in Kiska Harbor. The Navy provided the U.S.S. *Safeguard* (ARS-50), a towing and salvage vessel. Sonar scans were made of the harbor bottom to pinpoint and document objects. Diving teams from the National Park Service Submerged Cultural Resources Unit, Sante Fe, New Mexico; U.S. Navy Mobile Diving and Salvage Team One, Pearl Harbor; and the *Safeguard* explored and further documented the larger objects located beneath the surface of Kiska Harbor. One of the objects was the RO-65. The drawings of the sunken submarine were made by Lt. Paul Currivan, Executive Officer, Mobile Diving and Salvage Unit One, on his Apple Computer based on information provided him by the divers. Similar drawings were made of the *Nissan Maru*. A remote control underwater video camera was also used, and a video recording of what possibly could have been Jack Marks' B-17 was made. However, limited time and other priorities prevented a diving team from being sent down for verification.

The lamp (left) and brass porthole from the *Nozima Maru*.
DONALD McARTHUR

The *Nozima Maru* beached on a sand spit in Kiska Harbor.
After the war a Japanese firm salvaged most of the ship.
SUSAN MORTON

Photos of Japanese ordnance on the bottom of Kiska Harbor, taken by scuba diver Jerry Tilley. The top photo also shows a T.88 fuse in the center. JERRY TILLEY VIA DONALD M. ARTHUR

A Japanese ammunition belt
on the bottom of Kiska
Harbor. JERRY TILLEY VIA
DONALD McARTHUR

Porthole of the SS *Northwestern* which was taken from
the sunken hulk in 1974 by
scuba diver, Jerry Tilley. The
Northwestern, which was
heavily damaged during the
Dutch Harbor attack, was
eventually sunk in Captain's
Bay in the Dutch Harbor
area. DONALD McARTHUR

This photo is the same site
as the photo on page 169.
It was built by the 24th Field
Regiment, Royal Canadian
Artillery, during its stay on
the island. The top concrete
was removed before the author
took his photo in 1989.
JERRY TILLEY VIA DONALD McARTI

The Attu Morning Sun

RESTRICTED   THURSDAY 3 MAY 1945   VOL VI   NO. 99

BERLIN FALLS

12-DAY FIGHT ENDS IN RED VICTORY

WAR BULLETINS:

Soviets capture last of Berlin's strongholds.

Crack Australian division lands in Dutch East Indies.

Germans surrender in Italy

Hitler dead, a suicide.

American troops near Davao, on Mindanao.

Aleutian bombers raid Kataoka Naval Base.

British paratroopers land along banks of Rangoon River.

Seventh Infantry troops capture village of Kahutu on Okinawa.

KUHATU CAPTURED BY 7TH DIV.

Troops of the American Seventh Infantry on Okinawa entered and captured the village of Kuhatu. Local gains were made along the rest of the front.

The infantry attack was supported by heavy naval fire, heavy artillery and carrier and land-based aircraft.

SHIMUSHU RAIDED

Eleventh Army Air Force Liberators bombed Kataoka Naval Base on Shimushu Island April 30. At the same time installations on Kokutan Cape on the same island were attacked by search planes of Fleet Airwing Four, the Aleutian command revealed Wednesday.

CONFERENCE POSTS SET

Smaller nations were given important places in Wednesday's session of the United Nations Conference in San Francisco. Committees on 4 major points are headed by the representatives of smaller nations. Foreign minister Molotov will leave for Moscow soon because of events in Europe.

Admission of Argentina was one of the week's highlights.

Troops of the First White Russian and the First Ukranian Armies were cleaning up Unter der Linden.

Berlin had fallen to Soviet forces who viewed a scene of rubble and desolation Wednesday that reminded many of the veterans of Stalingrad and Sevastopol who had fought 1500 miles from those ruined cities, to their objective - the capital of Germany

Berlin, greatest city of the European continent and capital of the suicide Adolph Hitler's empire, fell to the Red Army.

It was taken at three o'clock on Wednesday afternoon, Moscow announced.

After 12 days of street fighting, from house to house, from building to building, using every measure of war necessary to their victory, the Red Army proclaimed the capture of Berlin - a word that belonged to the Russian explanation of Stalingrad and Sevastopol.

STALIN ADDRESSES FORCES

In a message to the Russian Army and Navy, Marshal Stalin vividly declared the "the center of German Imperialism and heart of German aggression," has fallen.

Pressing from all sides of the German capital, the Soviets crashed through the outskirts of the city supported by military knowledge, fire, and threw itself at the ruined capital."

Ruins were apparent everywhere but the German Volkssturm (civilian soldiers) and the German military ed every trick to hinder their tors.

The Soviets pitted their pledge of Germany's conquest of own homeland against that of the enemy and now hold Berlin.

RESTRICTED   SPORTS   THE ATTU MORNING SUN   NEWS   3 MAY 1945

DUST OFF THE PLATE

Softball leagues will be organized immediately after the completion of basketball league play.

Practises have been delayed due to the diamond being in poor condition.

At present the 8th Special diamond has been graded and may be used for practise sessions. The Navytown diamond is still wet but will be raked and rolled as soon as it dries sufficiently to permit work.

Gear will be made available at the diamond or at the Welfare Office for practise sessions.

Due to a limited amount of softball gear it will be impossible to completely outfit individual departments.

TUESDAY COURT RESULTS

The Shamrocks whipped the Trojans 45-17, Marines took the Cavaleers 41-19, and the Tenders beat the Boxwood, 34-16.

High scorers for the evening were R. Williams, Trojans, 16; Sims, Trojans, 13; Weichman, Box, 13; Lambert, Marines, 12; Ylvisaker, Marines, 12; Morgan and Labianca got 10 apiece for the Tends.

BOWLING SCORES TUESDAY

CARPENTER SHOP	Line 1	2	3	TOT
Pearson	114	148	159	421
Oup	171	131	127	429
White	167	151	180	498
Romick	187	148	194	529
Price	185	152	186	523
	824	729	846	2399

MACHINE SHOP				
Shriver	118	143	145	406
Reese	119	124	120	363
Caspano	202	153	143	498
Orient	141	173	193	507
Corly	142	147	160	449
	722	740	761	2223

HOT SHOTS				
Nowland	190	180	178	548
Valvo	171	162	166	499
Ardito	196	169	179	534
Carlson	112	172	201	485
Luhman	213	194	201	608
	872	877	925	2674

HARVESTERS				
Stone	189	181	159	529
Mitts	212	169	158	539
Rankins	142	172	138	452
Baake	184	142	162	488
Burke	163	203	195	561
	890	867	812	2569

SPORT SCHEDULE TODAY
Basketball - Barabara
1900 - FC-X - Aces
2000 - FC-Y - Fleet Wings
2100 - Boats - Ordnance
2200 - Trojans - Ball Is Down

"B" LEAGUE ENLISTED MENS BOWLING
2100 - (Navytown) - Av. Sup. - Yo Yo's

GERMANS PRESSED IN POCKETS BY ALLIES

Combatting units still holding out in Germany, British and Soviet troops to the north compressed the width of the German pocket to 63 miles.

American Third Army troops to the south advanced east 25 miles into Austria to effect a junction with Soviet forces west of Vienna. Moscow announced the capture of Rostock, on the Baltic sea. Also, south of Berlin, the Soviets took 120,000 prisoners from another pocket.

SPAIN REFUSES LAVAL

BARCELONA.—A German plane bearing Pierre Laval, Nazi-minded Vichy premier of France who is under a death sentence from the Free French government, attempted to enter Spain Wednesday. It was allowed to land, refuel, and ordered out of the country.

TROOPS NEAR DAVAO

American troops in the Philippines are closing in on the great port of Davao on Mindanao island after an 11-mile advance. The 25th Division on northern Luzon drove a wedge through the Jaranese defenses in the Carballo mountains.

30,000 JAP CASUALTIES

Lt.-Gen. Simon Bolivar Bucker, commanding the U. S. 10th Army on Okinawa, estimated that at least half of the original 60,000 Japanese troops there have been killed or wounded.

SUBS BAG 21 MORE

The Navy announced that United States submarines have sunk 21 more enemy ships in Far Eastern waters.

TRUK RAIDED AGAIN

Army Thunderbolt fighters of the Seventh Air Force bombed and strafed Truk again, sinking one small craft and damaging 2 others.

TWO JAP AIR RAIDS ON ALASKA IN SIX HOURS!

San Francisco Examiner — 6 AM EXTRA

VOL. CLXXVI NO. 155   SAN FRANCISCO, THURSDAY, JUNE 4, 1942   DAILY 5 CENTS, SUNDAY 12 CENTS

Bremen Raided by RAF; 4th Night Of Mass Attacks

STRATEGIC OUTPOST WHERE ENEMY BOMBS FELL

Planes Bomb Dutch Harbor Naval Base

Entire Pacific Coast on Alert; Further Thrusts by Nippon Awaited

American Mail Line
740 Stuart Building, Seattle, Washington

At Sea
Aug. 28th, 1943

Robert P. Patterson
Under Secretary of War
Washington, D.C.

Dear Mr. Patterson,

When you were kind enough on my recent visit to Washington May 29th to give me a letter of recommendation and travel authorization with which I hoped to continue the work I have been doing in Alaska for seventeen years, I recall your telling me that if it were not strong enough, to let you know and you would follow up with another one. Also on the same day you so generously gave me of your time, I went to the White House and General Watson told me the President's mind was that I continue my Alaska work as usual. Well—last week Admiral Kincaid ordered General Buckner to send me out of this area immediately and I am now on my way to Juneau, without even having been allowed to gather up many of my personal belongings including my lecture and religious films and motion picture equipment worth over $2000.00.

It all came about as follows. —Arriving in Seattle early in July I went to the United States Coast Guard headquarters, the Alaska Travel Control, and the 13th Naval District headquarters, and obtained all necessary identification cards, and the official permit, serial No. 227, signed by Vice-Admiral Fletcher to enter the Defensive Area of the Alaskan Coast. In other words I obtained all the papers I was required to get when I went to Alaska in January of this same year.

The Captain of the Mormac Hawk, a vessel taking freight and a Battalion of Sea Bees into the Aleutians, invited me to go along, and in my official capacity as Auxiliary-Chaplain for the entire area of Alaska granted me by Bishop O'Hara, wished me to act as chaplain to the four or five hundred Catholic boys on the boat. I held daily well attended services, also showed motion pictures and gave Alaska lectures each evening, and in other ways made myself useful. Naturally my companion of fifteen years in Alaska, Ed Levin assisted me. Everywhere we received the utmost courtesy from everyone connected with the Army and Navy. The Mormac Hawk Captain wished me to accompany the ship all the way as it seemed to help the general morale to have the diversion and recreation I was able to afford with my motion pictures.

At Attu, General Archibald Arnold and his staff, and in fact everyone on the island without exception were most courteous and I was very happy in the thought that I was able to assist by holding religious services and also by showing the boys the first motion picture entertainment they had since taking the island. Lt. Col. Mickey Finn at Holz Bay, a boy I had known at West Point and the real hero of the Attu engagement, said to me, "Father, the very presence of you and Ed here is enough to raise the boys' morale, because it shows that at least someone is interested in them."

All was going smoothly for two weeks and I was working very hard, when a sudden message requested me to appear at headquarters. I shouldered my heavy pack and walked from Holz Bay to Massacre Bay and General Arnold told me somebody's toes had been stepped on and I have to leave the island. At first it was to have been by boat, then came an order to leave immediately by plane at which I demurred as I have taken the stand that flying in the Aleutians is extremely dangerous. We left by plane, and before getting to Adak, ran into thick fog and clouds. For mile after mile we circled out of sight of land and at times were so close to the water (in a land plane) that the propellers were throwing up water on the body of the plane. Any sudden squall would have meant disaster. I am grateful to Almighty God that we finally landed safely in Adak. I reported to General Buckner and was told to see him and Admiral Kincaid the following morning.

After a few words with General Buckner he took me to Admiral Kincaid and the following astonishing interview took place. I bowed to Admiral Kincaid. He said shortly and gruffly, "I am sorry to meet you under the present circumstances. *You deliberately put one over on us!* Why didn't you report to General Buckner and myself when you arrived. *What you did could have been done by a Jap or Nazi spy!* This is war. This is serious."

I am sorry to say, Mr. Patterson, that I was neither awed nor too impressed by his heated words, but rather annoyed, so I answered, "Admiral, I am sorry for inadvertently causing all this commotion, and particularly so if I did anything unconsciously that I should not have done. I object to your use of the words, quote, *deliberately* put one over on you", unquote. First of all, I followed the identical procedure that I followed when I came here six months ago, namely, I reported to Captain Witherspoon head of Navy Chaplains and recreational welfare head, who came out to the boat and visited me there. He was the one who met my plane in Kodiak last Christmas, directed my movements there, and then sent me on to Dutch Harbor, and this time he told me to go to Attu as chaplain and recreational aide, and then return to Adak. I did not report to any higher authorities six months ago and was not told to do so this time."

Admiral Kincaid appeared nettled and angry and said, "you should have known better this time and reported to General Buckner or me. Why didn't you do so?"

I answered "Well, Admiral, I was expecting an invitation to meet you, when I was here three weeks ago. I am not in the habit of bothering important people." When he exploded at this statement I went right on, "It was this way. I autographed copies of my books on Alaska and gave them to the petty officer who first boarded our anchored vessel and asked him to give them to you personally with my compliments. I then expected an invitation to visit. Nobody told me to report to you but only to Admiral Reeves and he wasn't here then."

Admiral Kincaid then said, "I got your books and for all I knew they could have arrived by mail. The first thing I find was that you were on Attu and put one over on us. Remember, I have a one track mind and that is *authorization*."

"I am sorry," I answered, "but it wasn't my fault the petty officer didn't deliver my message."

He then briskly said "Give me your authorization."

I took out my wallet and handed him, —

(1) Your letter of May 29th, 1943.
(2) My Alaska Travel Control card No. P1254 of July 3, 1943.
(3) My Coast Guard identification 721522 of July 9, 1943.
(4) My Navy permit serial No. 227 for summer of 1943.

(5) My Auxiliary Chaplain authorization of Nov. 26, 1942, and valid for the Territory of Alaska for the duration.

Admiral Kincaid inspected all my papers carefully and then said, "There is no authorization to be out here. This limits you to the Alaska Coast."

I exclaimed "Since when have the Aleutian Islands ceased being part of the Alaska Coast."

He fired at me "You should know enough about military matters to know the Aleutian Islands are not the Alaskan Coast."

I retorted, "Well, I did *not*, and I am afraid I would have a hard time convincing an 8th grade pupil that the Aleutians are not part of Alaska.

Admiral Kincaid turned to General Buckner and said, "The fault was in Seattle. Send this man out immediately."

We all stood up, I shook hands with Admiral Kincaid and said, "Admiral, I admire a man who does his duty. You have done yours as you see it. I am sorry I caused this trouble but, — I did not do anything *deliberately* to put anything over on you like a Jap or Nazi spy. I am doing a public relations job for the American people, and in spite of this unpleasantness, I still intend to follow my policy of telling publicly only the good and nothing of the bad. I am not here to get any news scoops, but only use my right to comment months after the event on news already released. All I wish is to get human interest motion pictures that will effect what I effected in my last lecture season, — send the mothers, wives, sisters and sweethearts away from my lectures quiet in mind and even tranquil over their men folks in the war."

Admiral Kincaid still in a hard voice said "Get the proper authorization to be here and that is all."

So, — dear Secretary Patterson, I hope this account is not too verbose, but will give you a picture of the case. If General Watson has time to read this letter I would be grateful if you pass it on to him, so that between you two, I may get the credentials Admiral Kincaid thinks I need. Our conference was during the Kiska engagement and probably he was agitated over the total escape of 7,000 Japs through his expensive ring of steel around the island. After all, the personal chagrin of a few important men should be of less moment than the *sav-*

ing of the lives of many hundreds of our fighting men who found no Japs to kill or be killed on Kiska!

After all, I have faith in my Commander in Chief who sees the *whole picture*, and feel that the President was sincere in praising my Alaska work, and even when he asked me about the morale of the soldiers it indicated to me that he took it for granted that I should have access to them.

At the present writing I expect to remain at St. Ann's Hospital, Juneau, Alaska, until September 20th. I hope I hear from you there. At first I was going straight to Washington to tell you many things, — but, why not devote our efforts to fighting the enemy and not to quarreling among ourselves!

I was promised when I left Attu that my valuable camera equipment would follow me. It had not arrived in Adak when I left five days later. Major Luther Meyer, G-2, at Alaska Defense Command headquarters in Adak, wired me he is trying to locate the equipment. I requested him to send it by air to Juneau as soon as possible.

Being kicked out so thoroughly and ignominiously from the Aleutian Islands has involved a time element so that I would not now be able to return as I must prepare my lecture material in California. If it is in order and you can do so, I would be grateful if you could authorize my companion Ed Levin, who can remain up here longer than I can, to go to the various spots we have been this summer, — namely Kodiak, Adak and Attu and pick up my personal belongings. Also my King Island Eskimos are making two ivory cigarette holders for the President. I wanted to go to Nome and get them but it is too late now. Perhaps authorization to go to Nome could be likewise granted Ed Levin by you.

I await your letter to Juneau. In case you wish me to go to Washington wire me and I will go. Otherwise I hope to see you when I go East the end of October. Best wishes.

Sincerely and gratefully yours,

/s/ Bernard R. Hubbard, S.J.
St. Ann's Hospital,
Juneau, Alaska

December 8, 1941.

Major General H. H. Arnold,
Chief of Army Air Forces,
Washington, D. C.

Dear Arnold:

EXTRACT

*   *   *   *   *   *   *   *   *   *   *   *   *

Your letter of November 19th reached me only two days before the Japs reached Honolulu. They have not gotten here yet but we can expect them any day since we are nearer to Japan than Honolulu is and have less naval protection.

*   *   *   *   *   *   *   *   *   *   *   *   *

At dawn this morning I watched our entire Alaskan Air Force take the air so as not to be caught on the field. This air force consisted of 6 obsolescent medium bombers and 12 obsolete pursuit planes. Obviously, they would be of little value in protecting Alaska from destructive air raids. Furthermore, we are short of anti-aircraft ammunition and have a limited number of bombs, all of which are at Fort Richardson, although, in the absence of being able to get any elsewhere, I sent a few to Kodiak. So far our request for aviation gasoline storage has accumulated 20 indorsements but no gasoline. Another handicap which we suffer from is the fact that, regardless of many recommendations which General DeWitt and I have made, our construction up to the present time has been crowded into compact groups in the interest of economy in sewer pipe rather than dispersion against bombing. I mention these matters merely to give you a picture of our position should we have to defend ourselves against destructive air raids.

*   *   *   *   *   *   *   *   *   *   *   *   *

I fully realize that priorities in the delivery of aircraft may make it advisable to place other stations ahead of us, but if the defense of Alaska is considered at all seriously, it will be necessary for us to have more aircraft. Some months ago I wrote a letter stating that I would rather be reinforced by one heavy bombardment squardron than by a division of ground troops, since the only striking force that we can use is bombardment aviation and the enemy is always at a disadvantage when he is in the water and we are on land.

Most sincerely,

                                        /s/ S. B. Buckner, Jr.,
                                        /t/ S. B. BUCKNER, JR.,
                                        Major General, U. S. Army.

CERTIFIED TRUE COPY:
JERRY N. RANSOHOFF
1st Lt., Air Corps

MEMO TO: Officers And Non-   HEADQUARTERS FORT GREELY
        commissioned Officers   Kodiak, Alaska,
        of Fort Greely.   January 9, 1942.

    1. The Japanese are having temporary success in the Orient.
If they continue to be successful there, unquestionably they
will try again at Hawaii and probably for Alaska. The time to
get ready for this contingency is <u>now</u>.

    2. Wherever they try to land we must meet them and <u>destroy</u>
<u>them</u>. If they come by small boat to a beach or by a large boat
to a dock we must get there ahead of them by truck or by march-
ing. We must wait until they come within effective range, then
pour the lead into them by rapid, aimed fire. Every rifleman
must get the best cover available but must be in a position
where he can deliver effective fire. Deliver every bullet to a
Jap and deliver them wholesale. It may be that your position
may lend itself to tiers of fire. Machine guns, in general,
should be in positions to deliver overhead fire. When the enemy
is disorganized and the time is right we must dash in and polish
him off with the bayonet or disarm him and take him prisoner. We
would like to have some tenants for our new stockade. The Jap
is afraid of the Filipino bolo, and it is thought he is afraid
of the bayonet. He has had training in bayonet fighting and
is probably a good fencer. You are bigger, heavier, faster
and have a greater reach. You must learn to take advantage of
these qualities. You are on your own ground. He is on strange
ground and does not know the score. If the Japs come let's
teach them a lesson of terror that the whole nation will never
forget.

    3. After you have finished the first attack, reorganize
your squads, platoons, companies and larger units in good
positions prepared for the next attack should it come.

    4. Look to your physical condition, train like a football
player. Cut down your beer and cigarettes so you can run up or
down hill to the position that will give you the greatest
advantage in smashing the Jap.

    5. Corporals, drill your squads on your own time, if
necessary, to do these things. We all should be training all
the time, but boats must be unloaded, and guard and some fatigue
must go on. In spite of this, don't leave anything undone that
will promote your efficiency and training. Our best chance to
survive and <u>win a glorious victory</u> is for each of us to have a
quick, calm brain, clear eye, hard muscles, endurance, and an
indomitable <u>will to win</u>.

                    CHARLES H. CORLETT
                Brigadier General, U. S. Army
                     Commanding.

Lt. General John L. DeWitt,
Office of the Commanding General,
Fourth Army,
Presidio of San Francisco, California.

My dear General DeWitt:

                    E X T R A C T

    *   *   *   *   *   *   *   *   *   *   *   *

        I made strong representations to Captain Parker regarding the
urgency of our Umnak project. Talley informs me that the unloading of
transports at Dutch Harbor instead of Chernofski will delay his construction about a month.

    *   *   *   *   *   *   *   *   *   *   *   *

        Since the Cold Bay field is well along, I have directed Talley to
send the steel mat originally intended for that place to Umnak. By this
change the construction of usable landing field at Umnak will be expedited.

    *   *   *   *   *   *   *   *   *   *   *   *

        We have had very poor luck with our reinforcing airplanes. Of the
twenty five pursuit planes that started up, thirteen are now here and can
fly. Seven have crashed on the way and of these only four are salvagable.
Five are still en route, location unknown. Of the thirteen light bombers
that started, four have arrived here but can not be flown, due to gasoline
leakage, until additional parts are sent up. Four more are at Ladd Field
in the same condition. Five others crashed on the way up and of these only
two are salvagable.

    *   *   *   *   *   *   *   *   *   *   *   *

        The pilots of these new ships are very inexperienced, most of them
having had no training either in bombing or gunnery. Consequently, it will
be about two months before any of the planes will be effective for fighting.

    *   *   *   *   *   *   *   *   *   *   *   *

        During the past week we have had two accidents with our old planes.
The motor went dead on one of our P-36's and the plane crashed in flames.

The pilot parachuted to safety. Three days ago one of our B-18's had a motor cutout on the takeoff and was wrecked, killing one man and injuring several others.

      *   *   *   *   *   *   *   *   *   *   *

Next week I am sending some of our old B-18's and P-36's to Kodiak and will retain the new ships for training here. I have made some transfers in pilots so that we will have at least one experienced leader in each flight.

Most sincerely yours,

/s/ S. B. Buckner, Jr.,
/t/ S. B. BUCKNER, JR.,
Major General, U. S. Army.

CERTIFIED TRUE COPY:

JERRY N. RANSOHOFF,
1st Lt., Air Corps.

Letters courtesy of Hugo Laine, Buena Park, California.

March 31, 1942 5:15 PM

Telephone conversation between General DeWITT, commanding WDC and Fourth Army, and Admiral Freeman, commander Northwest Sea Frontier.

E X T R A C T

*   /*   *   *   *

Admiral Freeman. Well, we'll of course be very punctilious about that, we hope.

General DeWitt. Now, I have written this letter and it's along the line I have just talked to you about - along the line of the conversation just now. Now, there is only one question. What are we going to do about Alaska?

F. Well, of course everybody that we write to and get answers from informally agrees with what we think about Alaska. I just received word from Admiral King today, I have the letter before me. But they all tell the same story - that they haven' got the ships, and of course I think we have just got to keep pounding away. The British, of course, will help us out considerably in Southeast Alaska.

D. Well, I was thinking more about turning over to you any units of that 11th Air Force in Alaska. I was going to suggest this to you: we have 1 squadron of pursuit now, equipped with the new P-40 and we have one squadron up there equipped with the old P-36, but we have now at Spokane and are moving up there every day new P-40's to replace the old P-36's. So that will give us two pursuit squadrons equipped with the modern planes. Then we have 1 squadron equipped with the B-26, the new plane, and we have another group of ships being winterized at Ogden with - ships of the B-26 type, that as soon as they are winterized will go up there and replace the old type ships in the other medium bombardment squadron. When those ships get up there we will have four squadrons - two of medium bombardment and two pursuit, and one squadron of heavy partially equipped, that is with the four engine heavy bombers, but only half of them and the rest of the ships they have will be of the B-26 type with the medium bomber. My suggestion is in connection with that, that until such time - and we hope to have all the ships up there within the month - I mean all the new ships up there, Buckner is sending his pilots down to Spokane to fly them back so that inexperienced pilots won't take them up and won't lose any like we did before ---
When those squadrons are equipped with new planes and there will be more of them then than there were before, then the question be taken up as to how we want to subdivide that as between Navy control and Army control.

F. Well, that, of course, I think seems definitely sound, naturally, and the way I feel - of course I would like to have the thing in Alaska very much as we have it here - that we reach an accord. As I say, Colonel Hart saw the picture - we have been working together right along and he, in effect, deals out certain planes. Now, once we know what we are going to have, we go to town with those. We don't want to make any demands, necessarily, because everybody is short and we have got to make the best division and disposition possible.

D. But I think, Admiral, that we ought to do the same thing in Alaska as we are doing here. We ought to turn over a unit to the Commodore up there - Captain

Parker for his reconnaissance work over the sea. Base it either at Kodiak or any other place he wants to base it. But I think it ought to be the new plane rather than the old plane.

F. I think by all means, if you can give it to him.

D. Now, it might be interesting - I was talking to General Buckner over the telephone this morning and two officers are flying from Anchorage to Umnak today. They have a runway there 3000 feet long already completed and 300 feet wide. He was over there himself the other day. He was very much pleased with what he saw. They have done a wonderfully fine job and he has one bomber now over at Cold Bay, so those fields are getting into shape.

F. When do you think, General, that you will be able to turn over any planes to us in Alaska?

D. Admiral, I was going to suggest we wait until the new B-26's got up there. We can take action now but it would just be the obsolete type of plane that they have and they are not reliable. I'm ready to do it now but the new planes will give them their full allowance, of bombers, and they haven't got them now. A lot of them are out half of the time. That will be - well I would say within three weeks. I get a daily report from Ogden as to the winterization of those planes and they are all there now except four and about half of them are about 80% complete. So we don't wait until they are all done. We send them up to Spokane in groups of three or four and Buckner sends down and takes them up. As soon as he gets one squadron completely equipped, I think that is the squadron I think should be turned over to you or to Captain Parker and that ought to be within the next two weeks, I would say. Some of the planes have already arrived.

F. Well, that's fine General. Then I shall wait for further word, possibly from dispatch from you on that?

D. Yes, Buckner is going to call me back in two or three days and I talked to him about it this morning - so that we can decide on the squadrons - and I want to be certain that the squadron is equipped with the modern plane and they are all in good shape and complete. But he hasn't got enough planes up there to replace any planes that should go out. As soon as he builds up a small reserve - if he will I hope within the next two weeks - then we can do it. But I will keep you informed and the minute I hear from him let you know and give him the instructions to have it turned over to Parker.

F. Thank you very much General. I think I got the picture very clearly.

* * * * * * * * * *

CERTIFIED A TRUE EXTRACT COPY.

JERRY N RANSOHOFF
1st Lt, Air Corps

WAR DEPARTMENT
OFFICE OF THE CHIEF OF THE ARMY AIR FORCES
WASHINGTON

November 19, 1941

Major General S. B. Buckner,
Commanding General,
Alaska Defense Command,
Fort Richardson, Alaska.

Dear Buckner:

My Inspector, Colonel Hill, has just returned from his visit to Alaska and has acquainted me with your desires reference the additional squadrons you recommend for station in Alaska. Unfortunately, our commitments elsewhere and which have a higher priority at the present writing, will not permit us to follow out your recommendation.

Present approved plans contemplate that eventually the Army Air Forces in Alaska will consist of the following tactical units:

$1\frac{1}{2}$ Pursuit Group with 195 airplanes.
1 Heavy Bombardment Group (including long-range reconnaissance) with 68 airplanes.
1 Medium Bombardment Group (including medium-range reconnaissance) with 85 airplanes.

Conditions here as well as housing in Alaska will have considerable bearing on when these units can be sent to Alaska.

According to present estimates, the Heavy Bombardment Group should be ready for transfer to Alaska around March 1, 1942, It will consist of three Bombardment Squadrons and one Long-Range Reconnaissance Squadron, totaling 182 officers and 1,250 men. The Heavy Bombardment Squadron now there will also be assigned, making a Five Squadron Group.

The housing situation for this increment of Air Corps troops in March 1942 is causing me some concern, and I would appreciate learning just what you will be able to do in this matter by that time. If the housing there is going to pinch, then it is my plan to return the Medium Bombardment Squadron now stationed in Alaska. I might say in this connection that I consider it inadvisable to house any of these troops in tents. This whole matter of housing for future Air Corps troops in Alaska is being studied now. If housing will permit, it is my intention to leave the Pursuit Squadron which is now stationed there with you.

You are to recive a pursuit group of four squadrons which, with the one you now have, will give you a complete pursuit group, second aviation strength, of five squadrons with 130 airplanes. The time of transfer of this additional unit naturally will depend upon the completion of airdrome and shelter facilities.

Although at present no higher Headquarters is set up for the air units to be stationed there, it is planned to establish an Air Force Headquarters when all units are assigned. This will be preceded by a smaller Headquarters (Wing or similar) at the time the Pursuit Group goes up.

The tremendous expansion of the Army Air Forces during the past two years has made such demands on our experienced officers that practically all of the various Headquarters today are decidedly undermanned, and tactical units are limited to the bare minimum of experienced officers.

Pending the establishment of a Wing or similar Headquarters in Alaska, it would be of material help to me if you can arrange to use the present Group Staff for such planning, etc. as is necessary for your Headquarters, without taking them away from their normal group duties.

If you will be kind enough to let me know just what you can do reference housing of the increased load, I will appreciate it very much and be able to plan intelligently.

Wishing you success in this undertaking, which I know is not an easy one, I am

                              Sincerely yours,

                                        H. H. ARNOLD
                                        Major General, U.S.A
                                        Chief of the Army Air Forces

CERTIFIED TRUE COPY:

JERRY N. RAMSOHOFF
1st Lt., Air Corps

HEADQUARTERS FORT GREELY
OFFICE OF THE COMMANDING GENERAL
KODIAK, ALASKA

June 3, 1942

MEMORANDUM: To Officers and Non-Commissioned Officers, Fort Greely.

Japs have attacked Dutch Harbor.

We do not know the results of this attack. The Japs came a long way and we were thoroughly on the alert throught Alaska. We do not know the size of the Jap force but I believe that the advantage is ours.

We will very probably have an air attack here. From now on, until this situation is over, all observation posts and others charged with the duty of observation, must be keenly alert. The remainder of the command should get the maximum rest. Everyone on the post should sleep in his clothes with his weapon and ammunition at hand.

If an air alert sounds everyone must get to his slit-trench with his weapon ready to fire on hostile aircraft. As soon as an air raid is over, he must be prepared to join his company or detachment quickly and without confusion.

If the Japs come here, we are going to give them the whipping of their lives.

CHARLES H. CORLETT
Brigadier General, U.S.A.
Commanding.

"You Said A Mouthful"

Taken from a Joe E. Brown book

I'll never forget the morning that I left my house on the first leg of my journey overseas. For weeks I had been getting ready for the trip and thought that when the time came to leave I would be nervous and excited. But when the hour of my departure finally arrived, I was astounded to discover how calm and composed I was. I mentioned this fact to my wife when we were half way to airport. She took one look at me and said nothing—just turned around and drove back to the house so that I could put my pants on. A little later, however, I was safely aboard the plane that was to take me to the Aleutian Islands. Before I climbed into my seat, the co-pilot said, "Here's a parachute for you." I said "Thanks just the same, but I don't think I'll open it yet: It's a beautiful bright day and I'd like to get a little sunburn."

The motors had warmed up by now and we were soon in the air, heading out over the Pacific Ocean. And what a sight it was. I haven't seen so much water since the time my basement was flooded by a heavy California fog. History books are full of praise for that famouos explorer who discovered the Pacific—Personally, I don't see how he could have missed it. A few moments later I happened to glance at the instrument panel and noticed that we had gained an altitude of 14,000 feet. I began to get a bit squeamish and said to the pilot, "Is it safe to be up this high with a plane?" He said, "Yes, a lot safer than being up here without one." Then I asked him if he thought we'd get down all right. "Sure—we've never left anybody up here yet." He told me not to get scared because even if something went wrong and the plane started to stall, there was a radio on board. But that wasn't much consolation: If we started falling into the ocean, I'd be too nervous to sit and listen to the radio—no matter WHAT program it was.

We now began bucking strong head winds and I gave up the idea of smoking. I wanted to save what little gasoline I had in my cigar lighter in case the plane ran out of fuel. At 11:30 we had lunch, consisting of coffee and donuts. They were delicious and I ate nine of them, being careful to put the holes back in the bag. You see, like other war materials, holes are very scarce, so by saving the hole and sending it back to the bakery, they can put another donut around it. The pilot was telling me that donuts are standard equipment on all airplanes. In case of emergency the navigator can put two of them together with adhesive tape and use them for binoculars. I also discovered that by covering the holes with cellophane, they make wonderful sun glasses.

After an uneventful trip we finally landed in Alaska. It was so cold the morning we got there that the people at the airport waved to us with their hands in their pockets. I gave a performance that night out in the open at one of the army posts. And although it was thirty degrees below zero, not one of the soldiers left. I found out later they couldn't—they were frozen to their seats. The snow around there was sure deep. I noticed a sergeant standing in a drift up to his knees and I asked him if he wasn't cold. He said, "No, but I'll bet the corporal is—I'm standing on his shoulders."

The next morning, we had a wonderful salmon breakfast. You know what salmon is—it's a white fish that blushes easily. One of the Eskimos showed me how to catch them by fishing through the ice, and it was a lot of fun. Back home at Hollywood, the only time people fish through the ice is when they're trying to get the cherry out of an old-fashioned. We left here early in the afternoon for Dutch Harbor and arrived during the worst gale of the year. The wind was blowing so hard that we had to fill our pockets with donuts to keep from being blown out of the plane.

We had a tough time making Dutch Harbor because the wind was traveling 300 miles an hour and so were we, and we weren't getting anywhere. But luckily, the fog was so thick that we were able to chop steps in it and walk down to the airport. When we got to army headquarters we discovered the reason for the heavy fog: There were some Jap planes in the vicinity and the weather bureau had ordered a "White-out". After I entertained the soldiers, we had dinner and then chopped some more steps in the fog and walked back up to the plane. The next day, however, the weather was nice and clear as we flew to Kodiak. We were flying low and I got my first glimpse of a real genuine Kodiak bear. Ever since I was a kid I can remember those camera advertisements: "If It Isn't A Kodiak It Isn't A Bear." I also saw about 300 moose but we didn't stop, because I'm an Elk and there was no sense in getting into an argument. A little later, though, we did see a reindeer with beautiful big horns. The pilot circled him several times while the radio operator and I played the ring-toss, using donuts for quoits. I was very lucky and won seven out of ten. My opponent really shouldn't get credit for winning ANY of the games because he used powdered sugar donuts for tracers and I used plain ones.

-189-

USO Performers in Alaska

Edger Bergen and his famous dummy, Charlie McCarthy, performing at Dutch Harbor in August 1943. KHS, SGT. CLEVENGER COLL.

Martha O'Driscoll and Errol Flynn on Attu, 1944. KHS, SGT. CLEVENGER COLL.

Movie actress Martha O'Driscoll on Attu, 1944. KHS, SGT. CLEVENGER COLL.

Olivia De Havilland at the Attu hospital, 1945.
KEN TAYLOR COLL.

Olivia De Havilland at Adak, 1943. KHS, JOSEPH E. BELL COLL.

USO performers on Attu, 1944. KEN TAYLOR COLL.

Kodiak, Alaska

Views of Kodiak, Alaska, in the early 1940s (top) and 1945 (bottom). KHS JOHN TAYLOR COLL. (TOP), LOGAN ESTATE COLL. (BOTTOM)

Sign at Fort Greely at Kodiak.
KHS SGT. CLEVENGER COLL.

Liquor line at a local store in
Kodiak, 1941. KHS GAROUTTE COLL.

Three Russian navy pilots in
Kodiak in 1944. Russian
pilots picked up PBM (Patrol
Bombers) flying boats in
Kodiak, which were given to
Russia through lend-lease. It
was rumored that they paid
three dollars each for the
planes—one dollar for the
airframe and one dollar each
for the engines.
KHS VAN D. HESTRUD COLL.

Floating drydock at the Naval Air Station at Kodiak, 1941. KHS CAPT. BEACH COLL.

First pursuit planes (P-36) arrived in Alaska at the Seward dock on Feb. 20, 1941. AUTHOR'S COLL.

Richard Wood (left) and Fred Kennedy (right) on the firing line, holding M-1 Garand rifles Oct. 9, 1942. KHS CHARLES GUM COLL.

The army at Fort Greely advised Kodiak city residents to construct underground shelters to be used in case of an air attack against military or civilian facilities. Luckily no attack occurred during the war. KHS, THELMA JOHNSON COLL.

A .50 caliber, water cooled, machine gun on the top of the hill on Neimans Peninsula, Kodiak, 1941. KHS WALDO KICK COLL.

Target practice at Cape Chiniak
with a 1918 155mm Howitzer.
KHS JACK ALPERT COLL.

Dismantling the old kitchen at
Fort Smith, Cape Chiniak, July
1942. KHS

Unloading the captain's jeep at
Fort Smith, Cape Chiniak,
1942. KHS JACK ALPERT COLL.

Dishwashing duty at Fort
Greely, Kodiak, 1942.
KHS WALDO KICK COLL.

Guard detail at Long Island,
February 1942. The troops were
still using World War I helmets
and were issued new gas masks.
KHS

The photos on these two pages of the Dutch Harbor attack were taken by Hervey M. Thornton. He served as an aerial photographer in the U.S. Navy at Dutch Harbor from 1942-45. Thornton died in 1972 and his son donated the collection to the Alaska Historical Collection at the Alaska State Library in Juneau in 1992.

The burned-out hulk of the
S.S. *Northwestern*.

J2F "Ducks" at the NAB
Dutch Harbor. The J2F was
an amphibian floatplane in
Navy service since 1937. It
was carried aboard battleships and cruisers as a
"command" and photo recon
plane. A PBY is in the
background and a C-47 is
taking off.

Photographer Hervey Thornton. ASL PCA 338-563

Terrazzo floor design in the old Bachelor Officers'
Quarters at the naval station, Dutch Harbor. ASL PCA 338-768
PHOTO BY THORNTON

Mess hall at Dutch Harbor in 1944. Apparently war bonds are being sold. ASL PCA 338-590 PHOTO BY THORNTON

Constantine harbor at
Amchitka. KHS

Scow being loaded at high tide
alongside the USAT *Elina* at
Imuya Bay, Sept. 10, 1944.
KHS

Ships in Adak harbor.
KHS LOGAN ESTATE COLL.

Members of the 201st Infantry stationed at Kodiak climbed to the top of Barometer Mountain on Oct. 5, 1941, to practice talking on walkie-talkie radio to their commander below.
KHS, CHARLES GUM COLL.

Four members of the 201st Infantry pose in their position for firing a 37mm Antitank gun. They are posing off-duty, which accounts for the difference in dress. The soldier with the helmet on fired the gun, the one to the left, with face partly hidden, loaded the gun and the two soldiers to the rear fed the ammunition.
KHS, CHARLES GUM COLL.

Huts by the hundreds
were built on Adak
to house the thousands
of soldiers and sailors
stationed on the island.
DON HAZEN, NACHES, WA.

On board a ship en route
from Seward to Kodiak. The
Japanese-American was an
interpreter. KHS, REHRER COLL.

The NCO clubhouse on
Umnak when it opened.
These USO women came to
celebrate the opening.
KHS, JOSEPH E. BELL COLL.

A PV-1 Ventura bomber on Adak or Umnak.
KHS, JOSEPH E. BELL COLL.

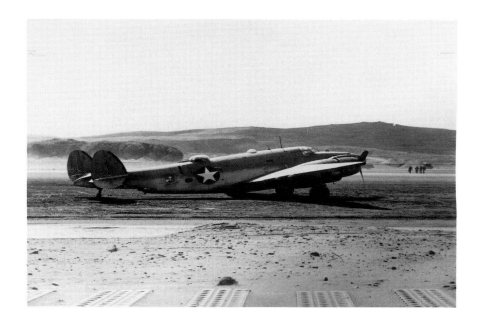

A disabled C-47 on Bell Flats at Kodiak in October 1943. The propeller mounts were being removed during salvage operations.
KHS, LOGEN ESTATE COLL.

A P-38 of the 18th Pursuit Squadron, 28 Composite Group on Amchitka.
KHS, REHRER COLL.

Capt. John Chenault's P-40E Tomahawk was part of the "Aleutian Tigers." He was the son of Gen. Clare Chenault of Flying Tiger fame.
KHS, JOSEPH E. BELL COLL.

A B-17 of the 36th Bomb Squadron composite in the Aleutians. A Cletrac used for the aircraft is also pictured.
KHS, REHRER COLL.

A U.S. Army Air Forces P-40 Tomahawk and a R.C.A.F. P-40 Kittyhawk in the Aleutians.
KHS, REHRER COLL.

A P–38 that didn't quite
make a proper landing on
Attu, 1944. KEN TAYLOR COLL.

P–38s somewhere over the
Aleutians.

A windbreak for engine
work on fighter planes,
Amchitka. KHS, REHRER COLL.

At the end of war on Attu an air show was put on. Shown is a P–38 (top), an AT–6 (middle) and a P–40 (bottom).

The Last Days of WWII as Recalled by Larry Reese

It was cold. The sea slapped the side of DD-411 and occasionally washed over the deck with a force that made you hang on for fear of being washed overboard.

We were sailing under orders from Adak, through the Bering Sea to Attu. Adak, was a ship repair station and supply port to take on stores and ammunition.

The Russian sailors who manned our ships under Lend Lease were being paid by the United States and making a great deal more money than the American sailor. This caused a lot of friction, however, we left Adak without conflict and headed west toward an unannounced destination that turned out to be Attu. From there we would head for the Kuril Islands that were held by the Japanese.

There were six other destroyers and cruisers in our attack force; three I remember were the *USS Trenton, USS Richmond,* and the *USS Concord.* Unfortunately, one man was washed overboard en route to Attu and lost in the rough Bering Sea. Our assignment orders didn't allow us to stop and attempt a search or rescue.

At Attu, the fog was thick and cast an eerie pall over the Aleutian Island port as we dropped anchor in Massacre Bay; the location of a fierce battle with Japanese earlier in the war.

We took mail ashore and stopped at the navy beer hall for some green beer, then back to the ship. We weighed anchor and left the harbor, under cover of night and the fog, sailing west. No doubt, the Kuril Island chain was our destination, but which island was not known. Soon, scuttlebutt told us it was Matsua; an island in the middle of the chain between Nakkaido and Paramushiro, which was one of the main supply depots for the Northern Pacific Japanese forces. This island was essential to the Japanese for stores, ammunition, etc.

Our target was the ammunition depot on Matsua. A surprise attack was scheduled so Japanese planes would not knock us out before we got to their dumps.

Following the fog banks in the Okhotsk Sea was necessary to keep our cover. On occasion, we would come out of the fog to find ourselves in view of a Japanese junk, which we would sink immediately in case they had radio equipment aboard.

Back in the fog we awaited the order to strike.

Before midnight we moved into line behind the other destroyers that were to make the run on Matsua.

The cruisers were laying off to starboard.

At midnight, we were in line and started making our run about 2,000 yards offshore of Matsua with all guns manned to strike. We were waiting for the fog to break so we could direct fire on the island. It broke just in times and we were ready to commence firing.

I had not been home for two years. I had been overseas for that time wondering what home was like. I was sure there had been changes from how it used to be. The faces in my memory of family and friends had dimmed, and here I was, a Gun Captain on a 40mm gun, ready to engage in something that could get me killed before it was over.

We commenced firing.

In a few minutes I saw what looked like the fires of hell. The whole island seemed to be exploding. Flames shot hundreds of feet into the air. My target was totally consumed.

As I continued to fire, I was too busy to feel the sickness from what was happening. The tracers assured me we were on target, and the explosions and flames left no doubt that hundreds had been killed. We headed east for the open sea.

Now, far away and looking back, we could still see explosions in the night sky rocking Matsua.

Dawn broke and the sea was fairly calm; as calm as the North Pacific could be. We were now far away from the killing field and somewhat at rest when suddenly General Quarters sounded. Apparently, all of the Japanese Northern Honshu Air Force was out to catch and kill the attackers. Our ammunition had nearly been expended on Matsua, and now we were faced with trying to shoot down what seemed to be the whole Japanese Air Force in the sky above us.

We fired what ammunition we had left at the enemy. Then our guns went silent. We knew this was the end for us. Home was never to be.

Then out of nowhere came our North Pacific Air Force.

A fight to save us was about to begin, and soon the sky was crowded with Japanese and American fighters.

Suddenly, the Japanese fighters broke off and headed west toward Japan. Our fighters didn't give chase but headed east. We yelled at our planes to come back as we watched our hope for survival disappearing into the clouds leaving us to what I thought was certain death.

The quiet on the ship was deafening. I could see the lost look in the men's eyes. The men I knew so well. I could read their thoughts. This was surely the end . . .

The mystery of the departing planes was understood when the ship's loud speaker came to life . . .

"Now hear this . . . Now hear this . . . This is your Captain speaking . . . The war is over."

—Larry Reese
Ephrata, Washington

Notes: Twelve Japanese bombers were within 10 minutes of our ships when contacted that the war was over. They dropped their bombs in the sea.

The cruiser *Concord* was credited with firing the last Naval shot of WWII. The 6-inch gun on the *Concord* that fired the final shot was transferred to a Philadelphia museum and is on display there today.

Tokyo Rose responded to the attack on Matsua saying we had killed over 600 civilians plus army personnel in this attack.

The *USS Concord*, the ship that fired the last naval shot of the war.

Six bombardments of the Kuril Islands are marked on the deck of the *Concord*. Three more would be added.

Sailors on the *USS Anderson*. Larry Reese is in the back left.

The USS *Brazas* (AO-4) was commissioned in 1919. In December 1941 the ship was engaged in ferrying fuel between the West Coast and the Aleutians. She spent almost three and a half years supplying Aleutian ports from San Diego, San Francisco and Seattle. In February 1945 the ship was sent to the Pacific theater until the end of the war and was decommissioned in February 1946.
HENRY VANCIK, YAKIMA, WA.

The 37th Infantry Regiment

The 37th was formed in March 1941 at Camp Clatsop, Oregon, with just two battalions. The 1st Battalion was shipped to Dutch Harbor and the 2nd to Kodiak Island, where it arrived on Aug. 3, 1941.

A third battalion was formed after the Pearl Harbor attack and was sent to Adak after it was occupied. It stayed on the island for several years.

The 2nd Battalion left Kodiak on Thanksgiving Day, 1942, stopped at Dutch Harbor and then was stationed on Adak until January 1943. It next made the initial landing on Amchitka, securing the island.

The battalion stayed on Amchitka until March 1944 and then all three battalions were shipped back to the states for training and assignments to other areas.

The 138th Infantry Regiment

The 138th Infantry of the Missouri National Guard was called into federal service on Dec. 23, 1940, as a unit of the 35th Infantry Division and stationed at Camp Joseph T. Robinson, Arkansas.

Immediately after the Pearl Harbor attack the division was ordered to the defense of the West Coast. Thirteen trains were assembled and the division conveyed to Fort Ord, California.

Early in January 1942 the 138th was sent Camp Murray, Washington. Here the personnel were furnished cold-weather clothing, and by January 15 regimental headquarters and the 1st Battalion were sent to Cold Bay, Alaska.

The 2nd Battalion was assigned to Juneau with detachments at Cordova, Gulkana, Teslin, Big Delta and later to Whittier and Nome.

On Feb. 3, 1942, the 138th was relieved from assignment to the 35th Division.

The 3rd Battalion was shipped to Alaska on June 1, 1942, and had been at sea for two days when Dutch Harbor was bombed. The convoy took evasive action and arrived without mishap. The battalion's units were sent to Naknek, Bethel, Umnak, Atka and Galena.

After almost two years in Alaska the unit was sent south in the spring of 1944 and inactivated at Camp Shelby, Mississippi, on July 20, 1944.

Operation Packrat

By 1947 army military units in Alaska received orders to pull back from the western Aleutian Islands. The small air bases built during the war were to be closed down. The facilities and materials of potential use to an enemy would be removed from the area. "Operation Packrat" was underway.

Because of the extreme Arctic weather, it was necessary, however, to keep some airfields open as alternative landing sites for civilian airliners that were starting to use the Aleutians as a shortcut to the Orient.

Shipping by sea and the use of harbors for cargo ships had a short three-month season—June, July and August. Only Adak had a deep harbor. Resupply to the western Aleutians was by BSP (Barge Self Propelled) or Sea Going Tug. They delivered emergency fuel and supplies to the scattered outposts.

Shemya Island, in the extreme western end of the Aleutian Chain was occupied in May 1943. It was thought to be a good base for B-29 operations against Japan because it was flat, unsinkable, and had a 10,000-foot runway. But captured islands in the western Pacific, with more favorable weather conditions, were used instead. Shemya Island was used after the war as a major stopping point for airlines on their way to Japan.

Despite all the advantages of location and availability, the western Aleutians were marked for a reduction to caretaker status. Plans were made to ship out excess weapons, ammo, oil, vehicles, etc., to points south. Estimates of usable stocks to be shipped out were from 80 to 100,000 tons.

By 1947 American industry had converted to civilian goods. Used supplies and equipment from the war were not in demand. A few salvage companies responded to the military's request for bids to remove the surplus items, but they needed to rent ships and crews to work under very harsh conditions.

It was planned to get items ready by early summer of 1947 or as soon as the docks and stevedores were in place. A black labor battalion was sent north to expedite the loading. They were responsible for the islands of Shemya, Attu, and Amchitka. In an ironic twist, some Japanese companies charted ships with Japanese crews and took off some of the supplies that were put there during the war to expel the Japanese from the islands. They were happy to get whatever they could for their war-torn country.

Hundreds of pieces of heavy construction machinery and vehicles were left over, sitting out in the Aleutian weather for years and subject to cannibalization for parts. They were practically worthless for reuse. When no salvage bid was offered or transport was available, items were burned or buried on site. The burning and burying in a sense, was much like a retreating army.

Operation Packrat was completed and for a time the western Aleutians was practically a no-man's land. But with the cold war heating up in the 1950s, the military moved back in with Shemya reactivated as an Air Force base. Attu had a Coast Guard base, and a major Naval Air Station was established on Adak.

By 1997, however, the western Aleutians had again lost its military status. Bases are closed and only the Coast Guard LORAN station in Attu is active. Airlines no longer need a stopover on their way to the Orient.

Note: The story and photos were supplied by Nielian O. Nelson of Argyle, Washington.

Adak in 1948, looking at the runway. The wooden walkways and guard rails were lifesavers during the extreme wind storms.

The Shemya oil dump. Aviation gas was kept in tanks. Heating oil and motor gas and oil in 55-gallon drums.

Construction equipment at Attu. Most of this was burned or buried as it was impractical to ship it out.

Barges and Sea Going Tugs were used to resupply the remote sites in the Aleutians and were also used to some degree to remove the surplus material after the war.

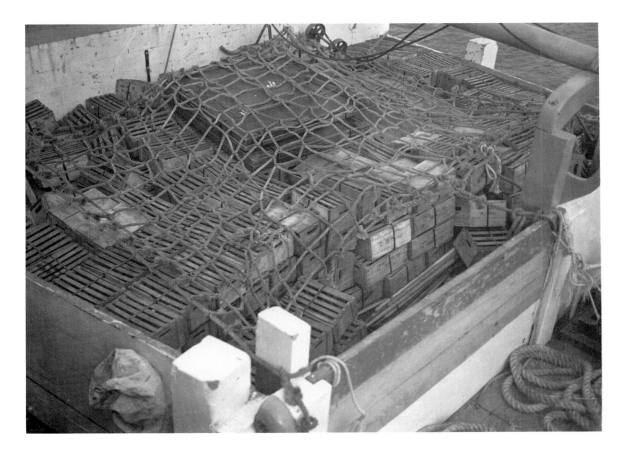

Salvage yard. Scrap sold for one to two dollars a ton at this time.

The lumber yard on Shemya.

Miscellaneous general cargo packages for shipping. Wood was salvaged from Quonset huts and the huge birchwood hangars built for B-29 maintenance (they were never used for that purpose).

Typical Sea Going Tug used between Attu and Shemya.

Mixed cargo ready for shipment.

The 86th Naval Construction Battalion

On Dec. 15, 1942, boat training for the battalion commenced at the Naval Construction Training Center, Camp Endicott, Rhode Island. Men from every state in the country were enrolled in the unit. The 86th was officially commissioned on Feb. 7, 1943.

The battalion left Rhode Island on June 25 for Camp Parks, California, and in July was sent to Camp Rousseau at Port Hueneme, California. Finally on Aug. 18, 1943, the unit was sent north on a freighter for Adak in the Aleutian Chain.

The unit spent its time in the Aleutians constructing runways, buildings and docks on Adak, Amchitka and Attu. Like many other units in this theater of operations, they had to endure months of remote, primitive living with rain, snow, cold and wind.

In September the unit was sent to Seattle and some of the personnel were sent to California to rain in UDT for the impending invasion of Japan.

INFORMATION AND PHOTOS COURTESY CARL REGGEAR, OROFINO, IDAHO

The smoke in the background is from the only bomb attack by a Japanese airplane on Attu. The Japanese Air Force in the Aleutians was no threat by the time the Americans took Attu in May 1943.

Mat laying crew on Adak.

Tents on Attu.

C.H. "Bud" Reggear as he appeared on patrol with his gun and fishing pole.

Shemya Island Diary

8-15-43. As the Troop Carrier plane (a DC-3 with twin engine, bucket seats, cargo tiedowns and a tail wheel) rolls to a stop on Shemya, passengers are offloaded and introduced to inbase transient quarters. Due to basic supply problems, these quarters are easily the more primitive on the Aleutian Chain. Located adjacent to the runway, they are little better than a tent, providing only space to throw down one's sleeping bag. On Shemya they went by the name De Gink. At the end of the line on nearby Attu, the 397th HQ & AB Squadron called theirs De Brass, which was generic up and down the Chain.

9-15-43. Devoted time to keeping tent upright—stormy.

10-15-43. Devoted time to keep tent upright—stormier.

11-15-43. Winter has slowed or stopped food deliveries. When the big, violent winter storms hit the Aleutians, nothing moves by sea, land or air. We are on the wrong end of the food chain here for four or five months. Nothing but canned Spam and Vienna Sausages. (Make mental note never to eat Spam or Vienna Sausages ever again.) In addition the Island has a frail refrigeration system, which often fails without warning. One day word came down that the refrigeration had failed and we had to pig out on pork continuously to keep it from spoiling. I have news for them; they were already too late. (Make mental note to never eat pork again.) At times diarrhea is endemic. Certainly it has no respect for rank.

11-20-43. The 372d Service Squadron began shipping out from Shemya, back to the States. The 400th HQ & AB Squadron assured responsibility for these extra duties. (The 400th is based midway along the south shore of the 2 × 4 Island, the long dimension of which lies EW.)

12-15-43. A short trip to the west end of the Island (Post HQ Area) would have confirmed the presence of the following:

713th Signal Aircraft (Early) Warning Service
37th Infantry
18th Engineers
Hospital Area
Navy Area
Bomb Alert Area
Gas Storage Area

12-25-43. Turkey was served for X-mas meal and the food was good for a change. Around holiday time the USO outdid itself in entertainment. A Group with Sad Sack performed; also Errol Flynn and Martha Driscoll.

1-20-44. A rare, beautiful winter day. The P-40 pilots staged a scramble out of pure exuberance.

2-29-44. On a mission takeoff, a B-24 ran off the runway at 715AM on a night-like morning. The plane crashed killing 7 men when a 500 lb. bomb, which had somehow become armed, exploded. Much of the action occurred near the line Dispensary. No one was killed in the Dispensary, miraculously. Other unexploded bombs were scattered randomly around the vicinity. In totalling itself, the B-24 clipped two C-47s (cargo DC-3s) and a B-26, which set between them. (The blast was strong enough to blow the door off our Pacific Hut.)

3-20-44. The Base Exchange has blossomed out suddenly with plenty of good candy and coke!

4-28-44. Spring is in the air. If one looks closely enough, he can discern little shoots of grass struggling up here and there.

5-14-44. Horseshoes have become a popular pastime since the arrival of Spring, judged by weather and not by calendar.

5-14-44. A trip to the Army Post Area on the west end of Shemya disclosed that the new breakwater has been advanced a great distance into the ocean and can't be far from completion. Likewise the parallel job of paving and extending the runway has been moving right along.

5-15-44. Our food is growing noticeably better from day to day. Today, a wonderful new treat—ice cream! Why are they pampering us?

5-29-44. Grand opening of a new theater, which is capable of handling 35mm film. At long last we have a chance to see relatively recent movies. Is this ever civilization?

6-10-44. Today the first Liberty Ship was nudged up to the new pier. The breakwater has again added a little more length. Still these works of man have yet to be tested by an authentic Aleutian winter storm. (Note: It has been a year since the Engineers waded ashore on Shemya with plans to lay down steel matting for an airstrip.)

6-16-44. From a very small beginning about a month and a half ago, there has been a marked increase in the number of civilians on Shemya. No women, of course. They established their area on a cross island road near the Post. (The Old Timers watch them preparing their complex and simply smile.)

7-19-44. Personnel of the 400th HQ & AB Squadron are starting to be reassigned out of Shemya.

8-19-44. Twin-prop P-38 fighters have replaced the P-40s. The dependable B-25 medium bombers have been displacing the B-26s. B-17 heavies have been history around here for a year. Now it's all B-24s . . . their original design specs calling for 300 mph, 3,000 mile range, 30,000 feet altitude. Of the nonmechanical bird population, the vertical rock clips on the north side of the island, facing the Bering Sea, are the seasonal habitat for myriads of seabirds. Puffins (the sea parrot) are particularly abundant.

9-19-44. The 400th has effectively been deactivated. Huts are nearly vacant. Some of the personnel were transferred to the 32d Service Squadron, which will take over Airbase duties; the others, dispersed to the four points of the compass. It is like the ending of an era, with the dawning of the new era predicated on the arrival of the anticipated B-29s.

This diary was kept by Lt. William G. Macbeth, West Linn, Oregon, a member of the 400th Base HQ & AB Squadron, stationed on Shemya.

THE Officers and Men

OF THE
400TH BASE HQ & AB SQDN.
REQUEST YOUR PRESENCE AT IT'S
2nd BIRTHDAY PARTY • SAT. AUG. 12th
Come at 2000 W....

• MENU •

SHRIMP SALAD   STALINGRAD DRESSING
CRANBERRY SAUCE   SOUTHERN ROAST TURKEY
SNOWFLAKE POTATOES CHERBOURG GREEN BEANS

CASABLANCA GRAVY   BAKED CORN
BOSTON HOT ROLLS   DRAWN BUTTER
        FRUIT PRESERVES

PIE-A-LA-MODE   COFFEE   HOT CHOCOLATE

    CIGARS   BEER

PROGRAM

Speeches by...

MAJ. BURTON A. HALL
C.O. 400th Base HQ & AB Sqdn.

LT. COL. BERNARD C. CARTMELL
Executive Officer to

COL. GEORGE R. BIENFANG
Base Commander

Music by...

122nd ARMY GROUND FORCES BAND

LT. WILLIAM G. MACBETH

P-38 pilots trying to figure out how to milk the only cow on Attu.

A skip-bombing target. The B-25s used practice bombs to make runs on this target as it was towed by tug out on the water. Photo taken in the Naval Docking Facility at Casco Cove in Massacre Bay, near Murder Point on Attu.

CHAPEL - 11-4-44 - CONF

John Fuller, air operations officer on Attu by a Weasel assigned to airbase rescue. Photo taken atop the pass between Massacre and Holtz bays.

The memorial in the foreground was erected by a Japanese delegation. It designates the high water mark of the Japanese counterattack, which was stopped by an engineering battalion on May 29, 1943.
ALASKA NATIONAL GUARD

CHAPTER NINE

LEGACY OF THE WAR

Reunions

Founding fathers of the Alaska Army National Guard, 297th Infantry veterans returned to Anchorage, Alaska, in 1989, nearly 50 years after entering military service. Some had not seen each other since the end of the war. ALASKA AIR GUARD

Veterans of the 11th Air Force who were stationed in Alaska during the war held a reunion in Anchorage in August 1990. This photo was taken at Kulis Air National Guard Base.

In September 1992 a memorial to the men of the Aleutian Campaign's 11th Air Force was dedicated on the grounds at the Air Force Academy in Colorado Springs, Colorado. This took place during the 11th Air Force reunion.

In early June 1992, a ceremony was held at Dutch Harbor, Alaska, to commemorate the 50th Anniversary of the Japanese attack. Many veterans, both civilian and servicemen were in attendance, including 85 former artillerymen of the 106th Coast Artillery Regiment of the Arkansas National Guard. Also in attendance were two replica Japanese aircraft of the type that attacked Dutch Harbor, a "Zero" and a "Val." ALL PHOTOS TAKEN BY M/SGT. ED BOYCE, ALASKA NATIONAL GUARD

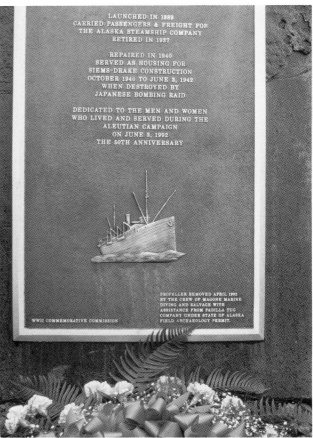

Propeller and memorial plaque to the *Northwestern,* destroyed during the Dutch Harbor attack.

Bunker overlooking Dutch Harbor, appropriately named Bunker Hill.

Robert Profitt, a Dutch Harbor veteran, explores the Bunker Hill outpost.

Memorial plaque on a bunker at Dutch Harbor.

In October 1994 the 11th Air Force Association held a reunion at the Air Force Museum in Dayton, Ohio. Several markers were dedicated to the veterans of the Alaskan campaign and captives of the Russians during the war.

This photograph, taken 50 years after the top photo on Amchitka, shows the same graveyard that the soldier is camped by. A deep hole was still in the ground, part of the gun emplacement.

CAPT. TOM CALLAHAN

The British Columbia Aviation Museum's World War II Collection

P-40E #1034 now on display at the museum. The plane was one of 15 P-40s diverted to Canada from a British order. After duty in the Atlantic off Nova Scotia, Alaska, and British Columbia, it was declared surplus in 1946. After many years of restoration, it is thought to be the most original P-40 in existence. This plane formed the nucleus of the present museum. DONALD MATHESON

A wartime view of Bristol Bolingbroke #9104 now on display at the museum. The plane was a Canadian license-built version of the British Bristol Blenheim bomber. The plane was sold at the end of the war and ended up on a farm for use in many functions other than flying. A new fuselage was added and the plane was restored for static display.

Remains of P-39Q #44-2485 which crash landed on the ice of Carpenter Lake, Northwest Territories on Dec. 6, 1943. After several attempts to salvage this aircraft in 1944, including the tragic death of two crewman of a Norseman which crashed at the site, the plane was abandoned and sank under 50 feet of water during the spring thaw. It was brought up in July 1990.

PHOTOS COURTESY OF THE BRITISH COLUMBIA AVIATION MUSEUM, PATRICIA BAY AIRPORT, SIDNEY, BRITISH COLUMBIA

World War II Remains in Nome, Alaska

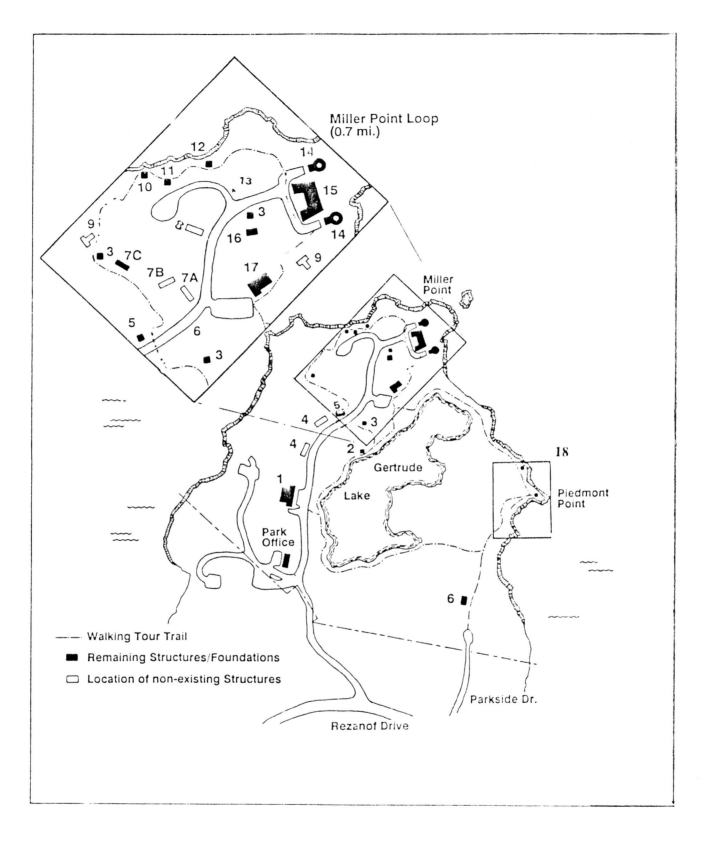

Miller Point Loop
(0.7 mi.)

Miller
Point

Gertrude
Lake

Piedmont
Point

18

Park
Office

Parkside Dr.

——— Walking Tour Trail
◼ Remaining Structures/Foundations
▢ Location of non-existing Structures

Rezanof Drive

Fort Abercrombie, Kodiak, Alaska

MAP AND INFORMATION COURTESY OF THE ALASKAN DEPARTMENT OF NATURAL RESOURCES

Fort Abercrombie, Kodiak, Alaska

1. War Reserve Magazine

This bunker held most of the ammunition for the 8-inch guns. The walls and ceilings were made of reinforced concrete 5-feet thick and covered with soil and twigs. Located a safe distance from the guns, it was hidden in the trees. Three 15 × 30 foot rooms extend into the hillside from the front corridor. The rooms contained explosive shells, powder bags, and fuses. Large ventilator shafts rise from the rear of the bunker.

2. Pumphouse

The house that stood here pumped water from Lake Gertrude to supply the fort. Old water lines can be seen at several places around the park.

3. Generator House

Five concrete diesel generator houses were scattered around the grounds to provide electrical power to the fort. This is one of the three of these small, one-room bunkers that still stand.

4. Warehouses

Two large warehouses, 21 × 120 feet each, stood at these sites. Level ground is the only reminder of both structures.

5. Storage Buildings

Several small storage buildings were built around the fort. You can see the remains of their concrete foundations.

6. Log Walls

Logs were used in the construction of loading platforms and retaining walls. Look for the remains at several locations. The wall below Piedmont Point is especially well preserved.

7. Garrison Area

As you follow the trail through a swampy area covered with small spruce trees, take note of the higher ground adjacent to the path. This is where most of the garrison buildings were located, including the infirmary (7A), recreation hall (7B) and the enlisted men's shower and laundry (7C). Twenty-five quonset huts were scattered throughout Miller Point to house the men; two more were located at Piedmont Point. The soldiers lived close to their work areas so they could be summoned at a moment's notice. Level spots of ground, about 16 × 36 feet wide, are the only evidence of where the huts stood.

8. Mess Hall

This was the site of the mess hall, the largest wooden structure at the fort. It measured 25 × 93 feet and could serve 170 people. A second, smaller mess hall was at Piedmont Point.

9. Elephant Shelter

Hidden in the woods away from the gun emplacements, the building on this site stored small arms and ammunition. It gets its name from the fact that it was big enough to house an elephant.

10. Searchlight Bunkers

At two sites on the seacliff's edge sit concrete shelters which once housed 60-inch, carbon arc lights. The lights were stored inside the bunkers and rolled out on grooved tracks. They were so powerful a straw broom held in front of them would ignite. They illuminated any dust or moisture in the air within 50 feet, creating a bright fog which made it impossible to see. Due to this, the lights had to be operated by remote control.

11. Observation Platform

This thick, wooden platform was part of a 65-foot tower. The tower was an observation post during daylight hours. It also served as a Battery Commander's post and as a base-end station for triangulating the position of enemy ships. Other base-end stations were on Spruce Island and at Spruce Cape.

12. D.E.C.

This acronym stands for Distant Electrical Control. Also known as pillboxes these bunkers contained remote controls for the searchlights (10). Large binoculars, mounted on a post in the center of the bunker, were connected by servo-motor to the searchlight.

13. Gun Fragment

This relic is a fragment of an 8-inch gun thrown here when the Army blew up artillery pieces for national security reasons during the Korean War.

14. 8-inch Guns

These 8-inch Mark VI guns were originally designed as World War I battleship guns. They were not intended for use on shore. The Army constructed special mounts to allow the guns to rotate 360°. The total weight of the gun and carriage was 103,000 pounds. Because of the weight, each gun had to be rotated every hour to keep it from pressing indentations into the track. These guns were primitive by World War II standards; the projectiles did not have proximity fuses that explode when reaching a target but had manual timers much like an alarm clock. The guns were fired many times in practice but never at an enemy target.

15. Ready Ammunition Bunker

Projectiles and powder bags were loaded onto carts inside this bunker and rolled out to the guns on either side. The maximum range of the guns was 18 to 20 miles, depending on the weight of projectile, 200 to 260 pounds.

16. Water Tower

This moss-covered, concrete structure was the water tower's foundation. The tower supported two wooden 30,000 gallon tanks.

17. Spotting and Plotting Room

This building was the nerve center and primary reason why Fort Abercrombie was classified as a secret installation. It housed the radar scopes used to target enemy ships. Underground cables connected the scopes to the radar transmitter and receiver across the lake at Piedmont Point. Thick concrete slabs extended horizontally from the roofs; these were blast protectors designed to keep enemy bombs from penetrating the earth and exploding next to the walls. The radar was used only in bad weather or at night. By today's standards, it was primitive. Four radar operators and an officer-in-charge were on duty in this building at all times.

18. Piedmont Point

From this area a 60-foot steel tower transmitted and received radar signals. Go beyond the D.E.C. and searchlight bunkers to find the radar tower's four concrete footings. Concrete foundations also remain of a generator shed, storage building, and transmitter/receiver building. Though Piedmont Point was home for the men who operated the radar tower and searchlight, no trace remains of the quonset huts and mess hall where they lived and ate.

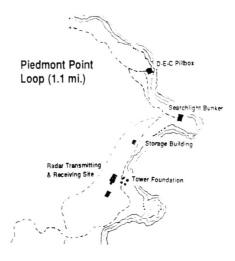

Piedmont Point Loop (1.1 mi.)

D-E-C Pillbox

Searchlight Bunker

Storage Building

Radar Transmitting & Receiving Site

Tower Foundation

Eight-inch cannon from Cape Chiniak, now located in front of the Buskin Inn, Kodiak.

Middle Photo: The Ready Ammunition Bunker. Projectile and powder bags were loaded onto carts inside the bunker and rolled out to the guns on either side.

Gun barrel at Fort Abercrombie State Park.

Reservists Recover P-38 from Remote Alaskan Island

by Maj. Ken Warren
(419FW Public Affairs)

When retired Air Force L/Col. Art Kidder (54FS — Aleutians and 96FS, 82FG, 15AF) got off the boat at Buldir Island Aug. 27, 1994, he couldn't believe his eyes. The P-38 aircraft he'd crash landed on this remote site Feb. 2, 1945, didn't look too much like he thought it would. Time had taken its toll.

Nearly 50 years after the crash, Kidder, 73, had returned to the island — located in the Aleutian chain off the coast of Alaska — with members of the 419th Combat Logistics Support Squadron, 67th Aerial Port Squadron, representatives of the Air Force Heritage Foundation of Utah and some Air Force photographers. They'd come to retrieve the aircraft for the Hill AFB Aerospace Museum.

"I don't know what I expected, but I thought it would look a little better than it did. It was the first time I'd seen the plane at ground level in almost 50 years," said Kidder, who had flown over the area twice at high altitudes since the crash. "A lot of the airframe was still intact, but the center section was partially burned out."

Recovery

The plane looked pretty bad. The weather has eroded parts of it and someone had used it for target practice . . . it had bullet holes in it. We were concerned about how we were going to recover it," said Sgt. Darrel Clarke, of the 419th.

Clarke said they decided to cut it up and palletize it. They manually pulled the wings to the boat and used the boat's winch to pull the other components the approximately 300 yards from the crash site to the salvage boat.

It took three days for them to recover the aircraft, which they then took back to Adak Naval Air Station, AK. It was then put on an airplane and flown to Hill AFB and later shipped to San Diego where it will be restored. After restoration, the P-38 will be delivered to the Hill AFB Museum where it will be permanently displayed.

Restoration Planned in San Diego

Retired Air Force Reserve Maj/Gen. Rex Hadley, chairman of the Air Force Heritage Foundation of Utah, a non-profit organization that locates and restores vintage aircraft for the Hill Museum, went on the trip. His organization paid for the boat and will pay to have the P-38 restored. It also obtained the aircraft recovery rights from the U.S. Department of Fish and Wildlife, as well as approval from the Alaskan Air Command.

"It's costing us about $425,000 to recover and restore the P-38," Hadley said. "But it's worth it because having it in the Hill Museum will help us tell the story of the 'Forgotten War.' I'm so proud of the reservists. We couldn't have done this without them."

"I can't tell you the emotions I felt when I saw that airplane again on the island. I'll probably feel a similar rush when I see it fully renovated. It will be a great addition to the museum. They're doing an outstanding job. This will help publicize an important part of the war that many people don't know about," Kidder said.

P38's Alaskan Mission

Kidder was referring to the P-38's mission over the Bering Strait during WWII. The Japanese launched thousands of "paper balloon bombs" the floated across the jet stream at about 40,000 ft. toward North America.

"They were loaded with two kinds of explosives — incendiary devices for starting fires, and anti-personnel devices, which were little bombs. Our objective was to shoot down as many of them as possible," said Kidder, "Unfortunately, some of these things made it to the U.S. In one instance, six people were killed in Oregon. Some even landed in Utah."

The Crash Recalled

He says he was on a mission testing the aircraft when he lost contact with his flight controller and eventually had to crash land the airplane because it was running low on fuel and getting close to its maximum endurance level.

"I was looking at the icy waters below me and spotted the island. I circled a couple of times, picked the best spot and went down. I hit my head on the control column, but I was basically okay." There was an Army weather station a short distance from the crash site. Its personnel rescued Kidder. A few days later, a Navy vessel picked him up.

"My adrenaline starts pumping whenever I think about everything that happened back then. I'm really grateful for what the Museum is doing to preserve this part of our history. It's really a fantastic, emotional experience."

(This article was reprinted from the AFB "Hilltop Times" and originally ran Oct. 13, 1994, in that publication.)

Art Kidder on Attu after his return from Buldir Island, February 1945.

P-38J-10
s/n 42-67638
built October 1943
assigned 11th Air Force
May 1944
crashed February 1945
removed from island August 1994
restored by Kal Aero 1994-96
placed on display at
Hill Aerospace Museum at
Hill Air Force Base, Utah 1996

Kidder's P-38 pictured in
1945 (top) and 1979
(middle).

The P-38 on display at Hill
Aerospace Museum.
PHOTO BY CHASE NIELSEN,
BRIGHAM CITY, UT

Bibliography

Benedict, H. Bradley, *Ski Troops in the Mud, Kiska Island Recaptured*, Littleton, Colorado, 1990.

Cloe, John Haile, *The Aleutian Warriors, A History of the 11th Air Force & Fleet Air Wing 4*, Pictorial Histories Publ. Co., Inc., Missoula, Montana, 1991.

Cohen, Stan, *Alcan and Canol A Pictorial History of Two Great World War II Construction Projects*, Pictorial Histories Publ. Co., Inc., Missoula, Montana, 1992.

_____, *The Trail of '42 A Pictorial History of the Alaska Highway*, Pictorial Histories Publ. Co., Inc., Missoula, Montana, 1979.

Freeman, Elmer, *Those Navy Guys and Their PBY's: The Aleutian Solution*, Kedging Publishing, Spokane, Washington, 1984.

Larson, Norman Leonard, *Radio Waves Across Canada and up the Alaska Highway*, Occasional Papers No. 25, Lethbridge Historical Society, 1992.

Long, Everett, and Ivan Y. Neganblya, *Cobras Over The Tundra*, Arktika Pub. Co., Fairbanks, Alaska, 1992.

Salisbury, Cliff, *Soldiers of the Mist, Minutemen of the Alaska Frontier*, Pictorial Histories Publ. Co., Inc., Missoula, Montana, 1992.

About the Author

Since graduating from college in West Virginia in 1961 with a degree in geology, Stan Cohen has had many interests. In addition to being in the ski business for 11 years, he has owned several other businesses as well as being both a director of a historical park in Montana, a consulting geologist and a founding member of the Museum of Mountain Flying. He now has his own publishing company in Missoula, Montana, where he lives with his wife, Anne. He has authored or co-authored 67 books since 1976 and published over 250.

He spent years researching the Aleutian campaign and wartime activities in Alaska and Canada. His other North Country titles include: *The Trail of '42, Alcan and Canol, Rails Across the Tundra, Gold Rush Gateway, Queen City of the North, The Streets Were Paved With Gold, Yukon River Steamboats, White Pass & Yukon Route, The Great Alaska Pipeline, Klondike Centennial Scrapbook, 8.6, The Great Alaska Earthquake* and *Highway on the Sea.*

Index

Alaskan, Aleutian History of Scouting Squadrons

Scouting Squadron 49 was commissioned at the Naval Air Station, Kodiak, Alaska, on March 2, 1943. Scouting Squadron 1 D-13 operating in the area of Southeastern Alaska, relinquished its planes and personnel to Scouting Squadron 70 and 40, losing its status as an operating squadron. At the time of its commissioning Lt. Cmdr. Carman Hawkins, A-V(N), USN, was appointed Commanding Officer of Scouting Squadron 49. Commander Fleet Air Wing Four assumed personnel administration over this squadron on March 18, 1943, at which time the operational authority and control over this unit was vested in the Commander of the Alaskan Sector.

Upon commissioning of Scouting Squadron 49, inshore patrol activities were conducted from the main base, Naval Air Station, Kodiak and from two advanced bases, one on the Island of Afognak, and the other at Sand Point. Each of the advanced bases operated with a complement of four floatplanes, six officers and about 15 enlisted personnel. Squadron administration was conducted from the main base at Kodiak. The Kodiak base had slightly variable complement of men and planes due to occasional aircraft accidents and irregularities in transfer of personnel. The normal complement was seven planes on wheels, eight flying officers, one round officer and about 60 enlisted personnel.

On or about May 16, 1943, the Kodiak patrol sectors were taken over by Scouting Squadron 70 and Scouting Squadron 49 was transferred westerly on the Aleutian chain to Naval Air Station, Dutch Harbor. All aircraft, officers, and enlisted personnel from Kodiak, Afognak and Sand Point attached to this unit arrived at Dutch Harbor by May 19.

On April 26, four planes with pilots and maintenance crew reported at the Naval Air Facility, Cold Bay from Kodiak. Routine patrol was maintained until May 5, 1943, at which time the four planes and crews were assigned to duty further out on the Aleutian Chain, two being stationed at Atka and two at Amchitka. Route patrols were conducted at these advanced bases from about May 15 to August 11, 1943, when all four planes and crews were transferred to Scouting Squadron 56 at Adak for temporary duty. On Sept. 14, 1943, these four Kingfisher planes with crews returned to Scouting Squadron 49 for duty at its base in Dutch Harbor.

The Kingfisher type planes were engaged in conducting routine inshore patrols consisting of one daily reconnaissance patrol covering the bays and inlets of surrounding islands and daily coverage by dawn and dusk patrols of the assigned sea-lanes. Training flights of all types, stressing instrument and navigation flights and also including gunnery, bombing and beam orientation were scheduled whenever practicable. In addition to routine patrol the squadron also carried on utility work involving ferrying of aircraft, transportation or personnel, emergency hospital cases, delivery of mail and films and delivery of medical supplies to Army and Naval posts.

A new development affecting this command materialized on Sept. 21, 1944, when Patrol Bombing Squadron 61 detachment was set up at Dutch Harbor, and this detachment was directed by Commander Fleet Air Wing 4 to conduct routine patrol activities heretofore covered by Scouting Squadron 49.

Then on Sept. 23, 1944, Commander of Fleet Air Wing 4 modified his instructions to Patrol Bombing Squadron 61 detachment by assigning that unit only one of the routine patrols heretofore covered by Scouting Squadron 49. The latter unit then continued to conduct one inshore patrol using Kingfishers, whereas the bombing detachment provided coverage on the remaining patrol with Catalinas.

KODIAK, NAVAL AIR STATION, MAIN BASE

Early headquarters for Scouting Squadron 49 at the Naval Air Station, Kodiak, accounted for 14 officers as pilots, including the Commanding Officer, one A-V(S) officer serving in the capacity of Administrative Executive Officer and about 70 enlisted personnel. Five Kingfishers on floats and about four Kingfishers on wheels were employed for carrying out operations assigned to this command.

Enjoying all the comforts and modern conveniences of home in the United States, Squadron officers and enlisted men found living conditions nearly perfect at the Naval Air Station, Kodiak. The officers occupied a four-apartment building completely furnished with modern conveniences including electric ranges and refrigerators. The enlisted men occupied well-ventilated and steam-heated spaces converted to barracks and located on the second deck of the spacious, modern and well-built hangar occupied by the Squadron. These spaces included a comfortable reading room for use of the men during leisure hours. The squadron officers maintained their own mess and all meals were prepared under the supervision of an officer, although this detail was rotated among all the officers. The enlisted personnel received adequate meals at the Station Mess hall near the hangar and also conducted a candy mess in the hangar.

Squadron maintenance shops consisted of modern well-equipped rooms in the hangar for the various shops such as radio, metal smith, engineering and storeroom.

The Squadron offices were located on the second deck of the spacious hangar and in addition to the usual offices there was a ready room for pilots.

All the squadron planes were stowed in this hangar each night and during inclement weather and all servicing of such planes was done in this hangar under ideal working conditions. Planes were fueled from gasoline pits on the ramp and excellent conditions existed for beaching of seaplanes.

SAND POINT, NAVAL AIR FACILITY

A detachment of about five pilots and about 15 enlisted men were stationed at Sand Point and four Kingfishers on floats were employed to carry out operations at this advanced base.

The four seaplanes operated by the Squadron were fueled from gasoline trucks. A small nose hangar limited work upon the planes to minor repairs and checks. Confronted with unusual operating conditions, the seaplanes were hauled upon the sand each night due to the inadequacy of the ramp at low tide. Engine changes and major repairs of planes were handled at the Naval Air Station, Kodiak.

AFOGNAK, NAVAL UNIT

A detaching of Scouting Squadron 49 was located at Afognak where four Kingfishers on floats were operated from Afognak Lake, located on Afognak Island. The usual complement consisted of four pilots and about 10 enlisted men.

Comfortable living conditions existed at Afognak with the officers occupying a well-furnished cottage and the enlisted men living in barracks equipped with showers, head, hot water and oil heaters.

Squadron operations consisted for the most part of gunnery and glide bombing practice, with a gunnery target anchored in the middle of the Lake. A few search missions were conducted from this Naval Unit.

All repairs and checks were handled at Kodiak Base and with no hangar space available here, all planes were beached at night.

DUTCH HARBOR, NAVAL AIR STATION

The Naval Air Station at Dutch Harbor was the headquarters for Scouting Squadron 49 from May 19, 1943 to Dec. 14, 1944. During this period there were approximately 14 pilots, including the Commanding Officer, Executive Officer and other department heads one A-V(S) officer who acted as Administrative Executive Officer as well as Personnel and Material Officer, and about 65 enlisted personnel. Seven Kingfishers on floats and two Kingfishers on wheels were employed for carrying out operations assigned to this command.

Squadron maintenance shops and operational facilities consisted of modern, well-equipped metal smith radio, ordnance and storeroom supply shops. All major overhauls however were handled at the Assembly and Repair Department of the Naval Air Station, Kodiak.

The squadron offices were spacious and modern and were located in the hangar. All squadron planes were stowed in a large hangar each night and during inclement weather and maintenance crews worked there on the planes under very desirable conditions. Squadron planes were fueled from gasoline trucks.

OTTER POINT, UMNAK ISLAND
NAVAL AIR FACILITY

After arrival of the squadron at Dutch Harbor, a detachment was set up at Otter Point on Umnak Island. A detachment of four pilots and about 18 enlisted men were stationed there, rotating duty with the squadron personnel at the main base. Four Kingfishers on wheels were employed at this advanced base to maintain daily patrol operations and to carry out other assigned duties.

Squadron planes were stowed in a large wooden hangar upon completion of the days operations, where nightly checks and routine repairs were made by an efficient crew of trained men. Major overhaul of planes and engine changes, except where it was possible to make emergency engine changes at this base, were performed by Assembly and Repair Department of the Naval Air Station, Kodiak. All planes were fueled from gasoline trucks.

Emergency supplies were available from the Army Air Corps although the Navy maintained a small supply depot on this base.

In brief, inclement weather interspersed with violent winds and heavy fog and snow storms limited the days of sunshine and interfered with flying operations.

The following incidents taken from the Squadron War Diary are indicative of the type of operations other than routine patrols and utility work:

KODIAK, April 30, 1943: Enemy submarine reported sighted in vicinity of Seward. Two planes were sent to search the area, remained overnight, searched the following day and returned. Results negative.

DUTCH HARBOR, June 11, 1943: Searched for Army transport reported lost. Results negative.

OTTER POINT, June 19, 1943: Searched for crashed B-24. Results negative.

DUTCH HARBOR, October 6, 1943: Two planes searched for enemy submarine reported by a transport plane. Results negative.

DUTCH HARBOR, February 15, 1944: Conducted a three plane search for a power barge believed to be wrecked in the area. The wrecked barge was located on Chuginadak Island and a rescue boat in the area was notified of the position.

DUTCH HARBOR, April 1944: Two submarine contacts were recorded during this period. Planes were sent to the areas with negative results. A survivors' search was instigated on April 19, 1944, in an attempt to locate personnel following the sinking of the *USS John Straub* southwest of Sanak Island. In addition planes were sent out on a search of an air operations plane with negative results.

Arrangements were inaugurated to withdraw this squadron from the Aleutian Islands under a plan whereby Catalinas from a Patrol Bombing Squadron Detachment together with a detachment from Scouting Squadron 48 were to take over all operational duties. On Dec. 12, 1944, the detachment from Scouting Squadron 48 relieved this command of operations.

In compliance with dispatch instructions to commence concentration of aircraft and personnel of this command at Naval Air Station, Kodiak, preparatory to movement of the entire unit to Seattle for the decommissioning of Scouting Squadron 49, six planes left Dutch Harbor for Kodiak on Nov. 19, 1944 and two more planes departed on the following day. Five planes and its crews remained at Dutch Harbor to continue operations pending the arrival of the relieving squadron detachment from Scouting Squadron 48 and on Dec. 14, 1944, these planes departed for Kodiak.

When concentration at Kodiak was completed the squadron consisted of 18 pilots, one non-flying officer, 88 enlisted men and 13 aircraft composed of eight OS2U-3's and five OS2N-1's.

On Dec. 24, 1944, all personnel and aircraft had arrived at Fleet Air Seattle from Kodiak and decommissioning was started. All planes were safely ferried to Seattle without any accidents or losses and all non-flying personnel were transported to Seattle via Naval Air Transport Service in an expeditious manner. All aircraft were turned in to the Aircraft Delivery Unit at the Naval Air Station, Seattle, Washington. All supplies brought from Kodiak or Dutch Harbor were turned into the Supply Department and all personnel received orders from Fleet Air Seattle for transfer to new duty.

Scouting Squadron 49 was officially decommissioned at the Naval Air Station, Seattle, Washington, under the supervision and with the assistance of Commander Fleet Air Seattle on Dec. 31, 1944.

BY WILLIAM ALBERTS, PASO ROBLES, CALIFORNIA

JAPS QUIT!

| Victory EXTRA | The Ladd Field Midnight Sun | Victory EXTRA |

VOLUME IV   LADD FIELD, ALASKA, TUESDAY, AUGUST 14, 1945   NUMBER 49

Accept Unconditional Surrender

Truman Announces Complete Victory To Thankful Nation

MacArthur Named Supreme Commander; Halsey's Fleet Stands Off Tokio Bay

Peace came to the world at 2 p. m. when the heads of the United Nations announced to their people that Japan had accepted the terms of unconditional surrender as laid down by the Big Three at Potsdam.

In the United States, President Truman made the announcement to the press after days of anxious waiting. The White House for the last two days had been open from 6 a. m. to midnight in an effort to make the earliest possible announcement. Happy crowds cheered the President and Mrs. Truman as they greeted the mobs that milled about 1600 Pennsylvania Avenue, jamming traffic that was snarled for blocks.

Prime Minister Attlee proclaimed the news to the British, who were wild with joy after six of the most devastating years in their history. Attlee declared, as did the U. S. President, a nation-wide two-day holiday.

The communication from the Japanese was received at Bern, Switzerland, where it was telephoned to the President. The announcement was made public immediately afterwards.

Following this was the news that General Douglas MacArthur had been named Supreme Allied Commander in the Pacific. This position entitles him to accept the surrender documents from the Japanese which will officially mark the end of the war.

While the peace announcements were being made over the world, Admiral Halsey's Third Fleet prepared to steam into Tokyo harbor, which will be one of the first cities to come under Allied control.

Casualties Reach 1,060,727 Total

Washington (CNS)—Total casualties from all causes for the U. S. Army and Navy since the war's beginning are 1,060,727, according to recent releases by the War and Navy Departments.

Army casualties include 197,676 dead, 570,766 wounded, 34,734 missing and 117,741 pws. Navy figures are 51,188 dead, 72,855 wounded, 11,611 missing and 3,756 prisoners.

Special Ladd Celebrations

All personnel, military and civilian, of Ladd Field, with the exception of a skeleton crew, to be determined by department heads, will enjoy a two-day holiday on Wednesday and Thursday. There will be no restrictions and no formations.

All squadron mess halls will serve a chicken dinner and free beer to all for dinner Wednesday. All enlisted personnel have been invited to a dance at Eagle's Hall on both Wednesday at 9 p. m. and Thursday at 9:30 p. m.

The Ladd Field radio broadcast, "Top of the World," presented each Thursday, is cancelled for this week. The program will be resumed the following Thursday.

The Post Theater will present James Cagney and Sylvia Sydney in "Blood on the Sun" as its feature on Wednesday and Thursday.